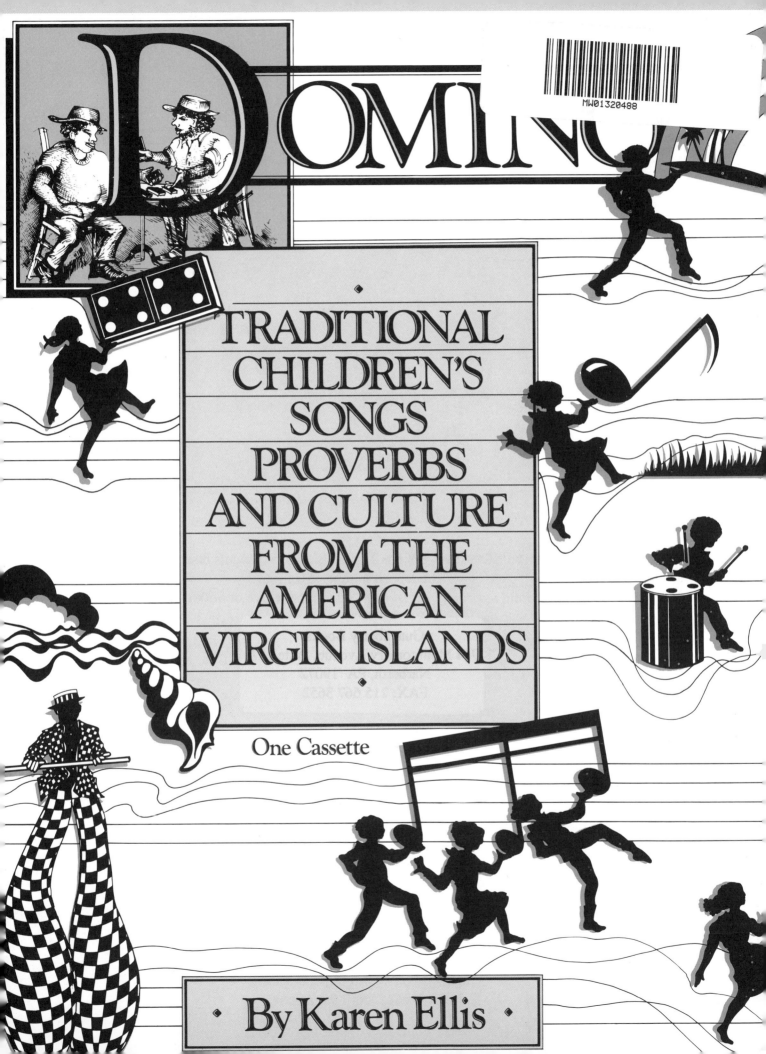

COPYRIGHT © 1990, BY KAREN S. ELLIS. All rights reserved.
copyright deposit number SRu 7-675
original field recording: Library of Congress, Archive of Folk Culture

Guavaberry Books
212 Gulph Lane
Gulph Mills, PA 19428
http://www.cyberpg.com

No part of this publication, including cassette recording may be reprinted, reproduced, utilized or transmitted in any form or by any means electronic or mechanical, now known or hereafter invented, including photocopying and recording, or in any information storage and retrieval system, without express written permission from the publisher Guavaberry Books.

To enhance your listening pleasure of the 35-minute Domino cassette tape
that accompanies this book, we reccommend using the Dolby 'B' or 'C'
buttons on your cassette deck.

Limited First Printing: 1990
Second Printing: 1990

ISBN 0-9625560-7-6 (set)
ISBN 0-9625560-3-3 (paperback)
ISBN 0-9625560-0-9 (cassette)

Foreword

When you fly into St. Croix, the easternmost of the U.S. Virgin Islands and the easternmost of any point of the United States, you will be approaching the island from the west end. If you arrive during daylight hours, at first you are going to see only the ocean and nothing else. Gradually the intense deep blue of the Caribbean Sea will become aqua, and then green. Finally, before you land, you see the sand, and the palm trees, and green, green everywhere.

When you land and walk around, you will find everything very peaceful. The air is fresh and invigorating. It feels light and clean; it encourages you to take deep breaths and absorb it within you. And you will be struck by the smells of all the flowers which are constantly in bloom: the jasmine, the hibiscus. You will feel a slight breeze, from the perpetually blowing trade winds.

Then you will look up and will see the clouds moving across the expanse of the open sky, always moving, always changing. There is nothing that stays in the sky overhead for very long. You may notice a squall in the water as you look out over the sea. And you will notice that it is raining somewhere where you are not — which could be five feet away from you.

The sun is very hot, very strong, and very, very bright. You have to wear sunglasses because you are going to squint. You have to wear sunscreen, because otherwise you're going to burn. The sun has an intensity that would be unimaginable anywhere else. Yet even in its severity, the sun is a friend. The extreme brightness magnifies all of the colors, exploding the sea and sky and flowers and earth with radiance and beauty.

When you wake up the next morning, you will hear the wildlife of the island: the birds and the insects, calling and buzzing in the bush. You will see some geckos, those small round-toed lizards, on your wall, and you will wonder what those little things are doing in your room. The geckos are soft and friendly (they can be trained to eat hamburger from your hand) and are very useful to have around, as they eat the tiny insects which otherwise might be annoying.

Altogether, everything is extremely serene and untroubled. It is a place one feels one could stay and enjoy for an eternity.

This is the St. Croix which I fell in love with, from the first moment I arrived. I felt a very deep sense of wanting to live there, a deep desire to return and stay forever. I did have the wonderful fortune to live there for a period of three years, during which time the material for this book was collected.

This book came from an activity I became involved in originally purely for my own enjoyment. The play of the children, and their unabashed joyfulness, affected and delighted me. I felt that the children and their songs were like gems I had discovered in my own backyard.

This book, this collection of songs and chants and games, is a taste of the varied and unique culture of the island of St. Croix. It is my small gift which I am giving back to the island, for all the island gave to me.

Philadelphia
January, 1990

KAREN ELLIS

Introduction

How This Collection Came To Be

In the fall of 1977, I took a job teaching elementary education at Ricardo Richards Elementary School, also known as "Strawberry School," in Christianstead, on the island of St. Croix in the U. S. Virgin Islands. This job became one of the most rewarding experiences of my life.

My assignment was teaching second grade, composed of children of ages eight to eleven years. My background included a degree in elementary education. I also had a certificate for teaching Orff-Schulwerk, which is a system of teaching music (primarily to children) involving movement, developed by Carl Orff in Germany during the 1930's. I had taught as a music therapist, using Orff-Schulwerk at the Philadelphia Child Guidance Clinic in Philadelphia, Pennsylvania.

Music was my hobby. All my life I had played music and been interested in music. Here on St. Croix, I became fascinated with what I saw the children doing every day on the playground. I wanted to interact with these children in a way other than the ordinary teacher-pupil relationship. And, by playing their games, by watching and listening to them, and by learning from them, I achieved this aim. For me it was much more satisfying and rewarding to build this rapport, to have this relationship with the children beyond my designated role as elementary school teacher.

At the start I would take my tape recorder, talk to the children, and invite them to perform for me. They would stand in front of the tape recorder and do one song after another. Day after day, that's how we spent our lunch hours.

In this manner, I collected their songs. These are the songs and games that the children sing and play in the schoolyard, in their backyards at home, that they'd play everywhere, like children do all over this world, as children play everywhere.

Songs and singing games are universal. Ethnomusicologists study this material to discover migration patterns, to see where people have moved to. The children's games go with the children. Wherever they move, they bring their games with them, and then the games get taught to the children in the region to where they've moved.

Many of the songs here were presented to me by a small group of children who taught me the songs, every day, at their lunch hour. These were girls and boys with names like Vernece, Hazel, and Roland. There was a core group of about ten girls and boys who gave their time to me; their pictures are included here. The songs were played by the children in the streets, in their backyards, in their own little neighborhoods, everywhere.

There were many children's games which I found being played on St. Croix which I knew were being played stateside, all over the place. I knew this because many of them were the same or similar to games I had played as a girl, or to games I heard in the schoolyards wherever I went. And then there were many which I had never heard of before. These are the songs which I have included in this collection.

Who Will Enjoy This Book

Any **teacher** who works with children who have learning differences (that is, what were referred to as "learning disabilities") will be interested in the techniques which I was able to utilize. The idea is to use the body as a vehicle for getting the information to the head. Knowledge can go into the body first and then go up to the head; it's rare and more difficult to go the other way. (Learning that goes into the head first usually never makes it to the body.) This is a vastly different way of teaching and learning that can help children who have learning problems, as a technique for a reading specialist to use. The classroom teacher, the music teacher, the music therapist, will all be interested. It is a means of helping to develop impulse control and freedom of expression, and feelings of self-confidence.

Any **parents** who would enjoy teaching to their children the songs and games of children of another land will be interested in this collection of songs. The songs and games are sufficiently similar to the songs and games played by children in the United States mainland to be easy to learn and fun to play and pass on.

Any **visitor** to the U. S. Virgin Islands will want a remembrance of the Islands, either to keep or to serve as a delightful gift. This collection of songs and games is a perfect example of the unique Virgin Island culture. These songs and games are indigenous to the children of the Virgin Islands.

Any **child-at-heart**, of any age, who wants to laugh and sing and have fun!

About the Cover

The characters portrayed on the front cover of this book are shown playing the game of Dominoes. All over the Caribbean — on St. Croix, on the other Virgin Islands, on Puerto Rico — people of all ages can be seen playing Dominoes. They sit on their porches; they sit in the sun or the shade; the men sit at outdoor bars and drink rum; all the people, all the time, will be playing Dominoes.

The sound of the players' laughter mingles with the sound of the Domino tiles being slapped down into position on the table-top: This is the ever-present sound. The laughter and the clapping are the same sound as the sound of the children playing in the streets, in the schoolyard, and in their backyards. It is to this joyous sound that I dedicate this book.

A Brief Political and Cultural History of the People of St. Croix

"Cattle minder know cattle temper."
> Literally, the one who takes care of the cattle (the cattle herder, or cowboy) is the one who best knows the nature of the cattle. If you take the time to learn about a person, you will have a better understanding of that person.

There is no doubt that the Virgin Islands are unique in all the world. Just as the beauty of the islands is special, so also are the history, the culture, and the people — both past and present. The lives and the history of the peoples of the Virgin Islands, interwoven with the political history of the islands, provides the background for the rich culture we see in St. Croix today.

It is impossible to comprehend the nature of the Cruzian people today without some understanding of the tumultuous history of the Virgin Islands. Since the arrival of European white men, the flags of seven nations — nations of white-skinned peoples — have flown over St. Croix. Yet today, St. Croix is populated for the most part by Blacks of African heritage, descendants of the slaves brought from Africa to work on the great sugar-producing plantations of the eighteenth and nineteenth centuries. The influence of the heritage and the culture brought by the early slaves is still very much evident in modern-day St. Croix life. The language, the traditions, the proverbs, and the songs of today's inhabitants are extensions of the African legacy, molded by slave life and, finally, life in a free society. The political and economic realities of the many phases of existence of the Virgin Islands all left their mark on the language, traditions, proverbs, and songs as well. By better understanding the political and cultural history of St. Croix, we can better understand the people who inhabit the island today.

Political History

"When man no like yo' dey sa give yo' basket fo' carry watah."
> If a man doesn't like you, he'll give you a basket to carry water. That is, he'll make your life difficult, or impossible.

Before the invasion of Europeans into the New World, St. Croix was populated by the Carib Indians. They had conquered and exterminated the earlier inhabitants of the island, the Arawaks, in the early fifteenth century. To the Carib Indians, the island of St. Croix was known as "Aye Aye."

Christopher Columbus, coming across the Islands on his second voyage in November 1493, claimed the Virgin Islands for Spain. The Spanish government, more intent on the colonization of nearby Puerto Rico, showed little interest in the Virgin Islands other than conducting an occasional raid to capture Caribs for forced labor in the Puerto Rican mines. The Carib Indians were exceedingly hostile to the white men; the Spaniards, in turn, hunted the Caribs in an attempt to drive them from the Islands.

Starting in 1625, Dutch and English settlers, plus a handful of Frenchmen, attempted to establish themselves on St. Croix. In 1649, the Spanish, exercising what they felt to be their territorial rights, attacked the settlers, driving them from the island or killing them. The French returned to St. Croix in 1650, took it from the Spaniards, and founded a colony for France. Three years later, St. Croix was deeded to the Knights of Malta. In 1665, the Knights sold St. Croix to the French West India Company. The French abandoned St. Croix by the late 1600's, and in 1733 sold the island to Denmark.

The other islands suffered through similar convolutions. St. Thomas was taken by the Dutch in 1666, then captured by the English in 1667, and formally returned to the Dutch in 1672. English settlements on Tortola (which the English took from Denmark in 1665) and on Virgin Gorda were periodically raided by Spaniards. In 1718, the Spanish again attacked Tortola and attempted to make a settlement there.

Under Danish rule from 1733 through 1917, St. Croix prospered. It was during this time that the great sugar plantations were developed on St. Croix, with fanciful names like "Diamond and Ruby" and "Judith's Fancy." Big mansions for the plantation owners, called "Greathouses," were built with three-foot thick walls made of conch shell and mortar, to withstand the hurricanes. By 1900, however, the world market for sugar had declined. The population of St. Croix was in decline. Many of the plantations, with their luxuriant Greathouses, were abandoned.

Starting in 1867, negotiations had taken place between the United States and Denmark to have the U. S. purchase the Danish West Indies, which included St. Croix. The Danish West Indies had become an economic liability to Denmark, and the threat of German occupation of the Islands during World War I provided more reason to relinquish control over the distant territory. In 1917, the United States ratified the treaty which established the Dutch West Indies as a United States Territory. United States citizenship was granted to most of the inhabitants of St. Thomas, St. Croix, and St. John in 1927. The Islands became a Possession of the United States, and were under the administration of the U. S. Navy. The Islands were authorized in 1932 to levy Internal Revenue taxes; in 1954, the Virgin Islands became a U. S. Territory. Since 1968, the Islands have elected a local citizen to U. S. Congress as a non-voting representative. The Governor of the Territory of the U. S. Virgin Islands was an appointed position until 1970, when Dr. Melvin Evans became the first elected governor of the U. S. Virgin Islands, as well as being the first elected black governor in the United States.

The People

"When yo' no hear noon bell yo' mus' hear turn out."
The "noon bell" is the lunch bell — time to break for lunch. The "turn out bell" is the go-to-work bell. This proverb may be translated as: If you ignore an easy order, you may be faced with a more disagreeable command.

The original inhabitants of St. Croix were the Arawak Indians, who were conquered and exterminated by the Carib Indians. The war-like and aggressive Caribs were, in turn, exterminated by the European settlers.

From the start, the success of the economic richness of the Virgin Islands depended upon slave labor. The first cargo of African slaves to enter the Virgin Islands were brought to St. Thomas in 1673. A census taken in 1688 showed 422 slaves on St. Thomas; by 1695, this was up to 623, and by 1715, the slave population was over 3,000. The ratio of black slaves to white adults on the Islands at this time was approximately eight to one. An unusually severe drought on the Islands from 1725 to 1726 resulted in the death of many slaves from starvation. The cruelty of the plantation owners to their slaves was renown, causing the King of Denmark to issue the order, in 1718, removing from the plantation owners the power of life and death over their slaves.

When the Dutch West India Company started bringing slaves to St. Croix, the Company obtained the slaves by purchasing them from their owners: the tribal kings and queens along the Gold Coast of Africa. These tribes had large segments of their population which were born and bred as slaves and thus were accustomed to following orders and knowing no other life than that of a slave. The white plantation owners, in consequence, received the impression that these African slaves would live and die without protest and that they expected to be treated as slaves, for they were completely submissive to their fate. However, as the slave trade to the West Indies increased, the African tribal kings and queens were not able to sell more of their own slaves to be sent to the New World, for their own stock of slaves became depleted. These tribal leaders then conducted warring raids on neighboring tribes, to capture the members of other tribes so that these people could be sold into slavery. These new slaves were an entirely different sort of person. They had not been raised as slaves; in fact, many of the new slaves were warriors, princes, nobility, and others of an aristocratic background. That is, when a tribe went to war to capture people to be sold as slaves, it would be the princes and warriors with whom they would be fighting, and the princes and warriors who, if defeated, would be sold into slavery.

Now there came to St. Croix a new class of Africans. Here were people who were not willing to passively accept their fate. They were accustomed to leadership, and had developed skills of strategy and organization. By 1732, the disorder and unrest among the slaves was growing, and in 1733, the slaves on St. John rebelled, massacring all whites and taking control of the island. It was nine months before the Danish settlers from other islands, with the help of the French, were able to quell the insurrection and restore white domination to St. John.

The slaves had used the techniques of their tribal heritage to organize themselves, including the use of "talking drums" as a form of telegraph, to communicate with slaves on other plantations all over the island. As a result of the repression of the slave revolt, not only were drums made illegal, but it became a crime to possess any kind of musical instrument.

In 1790, an insurrection took place on the island of Tortola, based on the rumor that the British government had ordered the abolition of slavery and that the plantation owners had refused to follow that order. The anniversary of the slave revolt is taken as a holiday today, in recognition of the heritage of the people. In 1792, Denmark did declare the slave trade to be unlawful, and by 1803, Denmark had completely suppressed the slave trade, and the last public slave auction took place. (The large round red-stone circles, where the slave auctions took place, can still be seen today.) Great Britain was to abolish the slave trade in 1808, and in 1834, abolished slavery completely in the British islands: 5,133 were freed at that time.

The Danish islands, including St. Croix, were a bit slower in granting freedom to the slaves. In 1847, the Danish king announced that all children born after July 28th of that year would be born as free people, and that all existing slaves would be given their freedom after a period of twelve years. Moses Gottleib, also known as "Buddhoe," organized a peaceful demonstration on St. Croix, demanding the freedom of the slaves. The Governor immediately emancipated the slaves, but as a result of his disobedience to the Kings orders, was forced to leave the Islands and return to Denmark to be tried for insubordination. He was condemned, then later acquitted. The slaves of St. Croix were freed, although their leader, Buddhoe, was deported for leading the insurrection.

"Yo' can promise yo' back, but yo' can't promise yo' belly."
> You can put off buying clothes for your back (you can make promises to your back) but you can't put off feeding yourself, that is, you can't make promises to your belly.

Conditions for the ex-slaves of St. Croix were not good, however. A Labor Act was instituted in 1849 to regulate the working conditions of the emancipated Blacks, but they were still forced to work in order to feed themselves and their families. A number of small insurrections took place during this period, in protest of oppressive taxation or working conditions, but it was not until 1878, as a result of a labor riot led by a canefield worker known as "Queen Mary," that true freedom was granted to Blacks of St. Croix. In 1915, the first labor union was formed in St. Croix, led by Hamilton Jackson; this union staged a general strike to protest the poor working conditions. Jackson was sent to Denmark to represent the labor class, and was able to gain some concessions from the Danish government, including full freedom of the press. A public holiday, Liberty Day (November 1st) marks that event.

Small Items of Interest

Alexander Hamilton, the first Secretary of the Treasury of the United States, was born in Nevis in 1755 and arrived on St. Croix with his parents in 1765 at the age of ten. He stayed on St. Croix until 1773, when he went to Boston. It is believed that the Constitutional requirement that the President of the United States must be a native-born citizen was introduced specifically to prevent Hamilton from being considered for the office of President.

William Thorton, the architect of the United States Capitol building, was born in 1759 on the island of Jost Van Dyke, now part of the British Virgin Islands.

Since 1967, United States currency has been the sole legal tender in the British Virgin Islands.

The tradition was begun in 1726 of granting a holiday to provide for a day of special prayer for protection against the hurricanes. July 24th still is recognized as a holiday, "Hurricane Supplication Day," in St. Croix. October 16th is "Hurricane Thanksgiving Day," a day of celebration and thanks for having safely passed through the hurricane season.

January 6th is known as "Three Kings Day." While not listed as a legal holiday, it is proclaimed as a holiday every year by the Governor of St. Croix, to celebrate the end of the Twelve Days of Christmas. On St. Croix, the big parades of the Christmas season are held on New Year's Day and on Three Kings Day. The parades include Calypso bands on flatbed trucks, with "moko jumbis" (the jumbis are spirits from the forest or the jungle who can play tricks on you) walking through the parade crowds on tall stilts. Many people dress up in elaborate costumes, and a Calypso King and Queen are crowned, awarded to based on the Calypso singers who had the most popular song for that particular year. In the bars of Christiansted, contests take place with Calypso singers creating songs on the spur of the moment, producing on-the-spot rhyming verses, relying on their individual talent and wit. The patrons of the bar "vote" for the winner with their clapping, for the Calypso singer who tells the best story, in rhyme.

Teaching Children on St. Croix

During my second year on St. Croix, I taught the fourth grade. Here the age range of the children was from ten to sixteen years old, yet many of them couldn't read or write or even speak standard English. I continued to collect the children's games and songs. The songs were now rhythmically and melodically notated for the first time, with the help of my friend Carl Bernstein, a classical guitar player.

The native population of St. Croix are called Cruzians. They speak English, although it is not always easy for a mainlander to understand the Cruzian speech. They have many words for objects and actions and feelings which seem quite irregular to non-Cruzian ears. Roots of these words and phrases have been traced to African languages. It is a dialect of English, a patois. The Cruzians also express themselves not only with diverse words, but also by having the order of the words be unlike standard English. Sometimes alterations in the word order denote time. The Cruzian speaker can, when telling of an event which occurred in the past, indicate by the word order whether it happened just this morning or happened a long time ago.

One of the difficulties I had as a teacher was in understanding the dialect, and one of the difficulties the children had as students was in understanding my dialect. Now, these children were required to learn to read by reading books that were written in standard English. Yet the children don't speak standard English. Standard English is a second language for them.

People who speak in a patois, or a dialect of standard English, have through their language separated themselves from the mainstream of society. Society essentially dictates that they speak standard English and write standard English. In order for these people to join in with the so-called "regular" society, such as the academic society, they are required to speak the language of that world.

Dialects which differ from the standard spoken and written language have come to be considered inferior to the standard language. Since the dialect is considered inferior, when the people speak their own language, we then embarrass them. In embarrassing them, we cause them to feel shame about who they are and what they are speaking. Their shame makes them feel alienated from and disrespected by the society they wish to join. It should seem obvious that when you shame and alienate someone, you don't give them any reason to respect you or join you.

It is very important for all peoples to have their own language respected. If it can be communicated that their language is colorful and descriptive and eloquent in its own way, then we can give their language the respect it deserves, and can then respect the people who speak it. These people will then feel more inclined to respect us in return, and will be more inclined to join in with our culture. The language of everybody everywhere should be respected.

In the elementary schools on St. Croix, even the children's books themselves were ridiculous. The stories in these books, which the children were being asked to read and to learn from, had to do with, say, snow, which these children had never seen and had very little concept of. Or there might be a story involving a train, and none of the children had ever seen a train. Many, or most, of the children who grew up on one side of the island, in Frederickstead, never left that town. They were never even taken to see Christianstead, a few miles down the road. They had a comparatively isolated upbringing. The material they were being asked to read did not reflect the environment in which these children grew up.

In schools on the mainland, teaching English as a second language is considered relevant and real. But here I was on St. Croix, being expected to teach English as though there were no language problem at all. As a result of this narrow attitude, there were many children in my classes who were a couple of years behind in their reading level.

Spelling was very difficult for the Cruzian children, as they don't pronounce words with the same tones and inflections as used in standard English. And, certainly, teaching spelling to standard-English-speaking children is difficult enough! For instance, if a student wanted to say the word "mouth," she might pronounce the word as "mout." She wouldn't say "mouth" because the final "th" sound is not present in the Cruzian dialect.

Every child needs to know how to talk before he or she can learn to read. The rudiment of talking is chanting. All babies are sung to or chanted to, for this is the beginning of the language experience which each baby has. Those early language experiences create reading readiness. Here on St. Croix, the verbal skills of the children were under-developed simply because these children were not encouraged to carry on conversations with their elders. They were basically expected to listen and to do what they were told to do and be obedient but not really engage in a lot of descriptive conversation. This is a cultural difference. Parents did not elicit a lot of descriptive discussion from their children, but, in the schools, the children were expected to have these verbal skills. Their talents were in their songs and in their chants, which is their living poetry. And so I decided to create my link with these children and establish an understanding with them based upon what they knew, upon their verbal skills, their culture, their world.

These are the grounds under which I resolved to develop my own technique for teaching reading. One day, in the fourth grade class, I took the reading books away. I began to draw upon the techniques which I had learned in Orff-Schulwerk. I started first by using the songs and games which I had picked up on the playground. To learn to read and write English, the children would have to develop a keen ear for listening. The English that they were required to learn was a different language than the language they spoke, so they really had to listen carefully.

First I wrote sentences on the blackboard, sentences in standard English, such as "What time is it?" Below this, I would write a phrase or sentence in the Cruzian dialect. Then I asked the students to differentiate which one was which, and to point out the differences between the two sentences. I wrote the Cruzian dialect just as they said it, with "dem" for "them," for example. That was the beginning of how I realized that the children were *not* aware of the differences. They were not aware of what I was speaking as being standard English and what they were speaking as being a dialect. So we began, fresh, on that basis.

I moved then into ear training. Using ear training, I asked my class to watch what I did and to echo the sounds I made. I would clap a rhythm, then have them repeat the pattern back to me. In this way, they were forced to develop their listening skills. They also had to develop their coordination, in order to clap. Not that they couldn't clap — of course they could clap — but some children didn't necessarily know when to stop, or how to add an accented clap with the right timing. Many times when we were clapping together, it would be the children who were the slow learners who would not clap the pattern correctly or wouldn't stop clapping when everyone else did. These children would in this case obtain immediate feedback from the rest of the class, because, instead of stopping at the right time, they were clapping when they weren't supposed to be. Their classmates would look at them, and the culprits would get embarrassed.

One of the elements which is crucial in every child's development is mastery over his or her body. If you think about an equivalent situation for an adult — to not have control of his or her body — it is a highly awkward and embarrassing condition. With the ear training exercises, we had a very strong motivation for children to want to listen: to avoid personal embarrassment and also to master coordination.

The rhythms which I clapped out were, at first, not the rhythms from their games. At first, they were just simple, ordinary rhythms. Beginning with one measure, I then expanded the clapping to two measures. We'd start with four even counts: TA TA TA TA. Then I'd place an accent on the first beat: <u>TA</u> Ti Ti Ti, <u>TA</u> Ti Ti Ti. Then more complex, a syncopated rhythm: <u>TA</u> TiTi <u>TA</u> <u>TA</u>, TiTi TiTi <u>TA</u> <u>TA</u>.

When the students clapped the rhythm back to me, they'd have to respond absolutely correctly. If a student wasn't right on the money, the other members of the class would look at the offender, and point or laugh. And it was obvious — there could be no deception; a student couldn't say "Oh, I did too hear you!" or "Oh, I did too clap that right!" It was obvious that either they were "there" or they weren't. They were very motivated to be "there" because the children didn't want to be embarrassed, for there was a great deal of peer pressure to perform well. The students acquired a tremendous amount of inspiration, as a demand which they put upon themselves. Here the students were excited by themselves and by each other, and were not being dependant on the teacher for motivation or specific encouragement. This was the miracle of utilizing this technique.

I expanded the clapping to make longer measures and to include more intricate rhythms, and the class learned to keep up and do well with these elaborate rhythms. I then added some fun by splitting the room into two parts and having the children clap rondos: First one group, then the other, as a round. We then created more complex, physically demanding activities by involving more than clapping, by incorporating other body parts. I included in the rhythmic structure initially clapping hands, then snapping fingers, and then stamping their feet and patchen, which is slapping the thighs with the hands. Finally, we added the voice. Eventually, I had to devise rhythms and actions which involved all my body parts and the class would have to do the same actions in the same rhythms back to me. It became very intense, a lot of fun, very absorbing, and a challenge — a challenge at which every student wanted to do well.

When this was recognized as the activity the class came to expect, and when everybody was doing well at it, I said, "Now, who can tell me what this is?" And for the first time, I clapped out, from beginning to end, the rhythmic pattern of one of their playground songs. Immediately, the students caught on, and someone shouted, "Hey, that's 'Domino'." The children quickly recognized the songs I clapped, as these songs were part of the everyday world in which they lived. The songs were already a part of the children's knowledge.

The classroom excitement kept building with each passing day. The children instinctively felt that they were accomplishing something of great importance in their lives. The word was out around the schoolyard — students from other classes would try to hang out in our room to hear and see what was going on. It was tremendously stimulating.

After the class got accustomed to me clapping out the rhythm of the words of their songs, I then split the class into two groups, as we had done earlier. One group would start clapping the song and the other group would come in at the right point, to make a round out of the songs — just to make it complicated, and just to make it fun.

At the conclusion of doing these rounds and having fun in this way a couple of times, I then told the class that I wanted them to write the words to that song. The class was shocked. It had never occurred to them before that they could write the words for something *which they already knew*. Up to that time, their writing experience had been made up of dealing with subjects which were foreign and lifeless. Now the paper and the pencils were poised as the students began to think about what they had to do, and they started to write. For the first time, they really cared about how a word was spelled. They wanted to write the song — *their* song — perfectly. Everyone ran from one person to the other to see who could help them spell a particular word. The students were each, in fact, building his or her own songbook. They were writing out their own poetry. At the end of every week, they had committed that week's songs and games to memory. They had to write the songs for me, and this became their spelling test. In this way, each student learned how to spell.

At the start, the children were not able to write out the songs which normally they sang. I'd clap out a song — say, "Domino." The students would guess the name of the song, and I'd say, "Okay, now write it." The class would start screaming, because how do you spell the word "Domino"? They wanted to know. Some songs contained some very hard words for students of this age, but they really wanted to learn how to spell. The clapping and writing of the songs became their language arts exercise, their spelling exercise, and their reading program.

Before long, we worked on standard English verses of the songs, so when the children wrote the words, they did their best to write in standard English. In effect, in the process of writing the words, the children were translating from Cruzian, their native language, to English.

As an art project, each child was given a six-foot length of paper. Then they copied all the words to the songs from the notebooks we'd been keeping, and each child drew pictures, whatever he or she thought would be an appropriate picture. We took these scrolls out in the hallway and taped them to the wall outside the classroom. The other children walking down the hall were captivated by these pictures — the pictures were colorful — then began to realize what they were looking at (only playground songs, not a story from a book!) and they too found that they could read and comprehend the words. Because they could say the words, because they knew the songs, they could read those words.

At the end of the year, when I evaluated their reading levels, the children had risen two or three years in their reading level skills. Our activities had that kind of impact. It was a particularly successful teaching method for those children who had been reading below grade level.

Further Notes on the Songs in this Collection

The songs and games in this collection represent something much more than just the music and the words printed on the pages. These songs are the capture of living poetry. In the life of the children who sing and play, the songs are always changing, never static. A child arrives from another part of the island and adds another word, and an improvisation is born. Even though there is a basic core to each song which the people learn and memorize as part of their childhood, they also are free to improvise on the basic core, to add and subtract as they feel like it. And the song changes, from one year to the next, from one generation to the next.

Recording the songs, being involved in the singing and the playing, and seeing the life and the changes in the songs is very exciting. It is the beginning of speech; it is the poetry of children. This is the culture of the children. And it is a culture of which they are extremely proud.

Reggae music, made popular in the mainland United States over the past fifteen years, is the rhythm of the island of Jamaica. The rhythms of the Virgin Islands form what we know as Calypso.

The songs in this book may seem to be familiar and appear to be similar to standard mainland United States children's songs. But the way they are played — the motions and the rhythms — are unique.

How to Use This Book

All the movements which accompany each song are written down on the page with that song. You will see the order in which to do the movements, and the musical notation will indicate the rhythm in which the movements are performed.

To learn any of the songs and games presented in this book, the best way to get oriented is to first read the instructions and learn each action. Then memorize the order (the sequence) in which the actions are played. Finally, you're ready to learn the song or the chant. If you can't read music, or hate to read music, or just don't feel like reading the music, you can always listen to the tape. It is designed to help you learn, no matter what your level of formal music accomplishment.

There is a legend at the top of each page which indicates what movements are involved in the song on that page and gives you an idea as to how complicated it is. If it's just a jump-rope chant, you will see a symbol of two children jumping rope. If it's a clap pattern, you'll see two little hands. There is a symbol for line-dancing songs; a symbol for songs with movements of the hips; a symbol with two little feet which indicates foot motion is involved. The symbol of a circle with a "G" in the center indicates a Circle Game. The letters "C + R" signify a Call and Response game.

The songs in this book require varying levels of ability to learn the song and its motions, from first grade on up. Of course, adults may have trouble with some of these songs, depending on how physically oriented they are. If you have trouble, get your kids to help you!

In the photographs, you will see children with their hands performing certain motions. Underneath those pictures, I have labels indicating what that motion is called. Throughout the book, if a motion is referred to as "Clap Sky Ground," you can look at the photographs to see what "Clap Sky Ground" means.

Songs that are not sung but are said are called chants. The music notation indicates that these are chants because there are no heads on the musical notes, just the stems of the notes to illustrate the rhythm of the chant.

The words to the songs here are written in a mixture of standard English and Cruzian. When certain words are written in Cruzian, it is because that is what was most appropriate. Many times, the songs and chants are sung in standard English, just the way that you or I would say it.

Remember, the idea of playing music is to have fun with it, because you don't "work" music, you *play* it. The whole notion is to play, and to have fun. There is a universal aspect to all children's songs, an aspect of amusement and of silliness. The elements of children's play are sacred. The enactment is joyous.

Acknowledgements

Thanks to:

All of the children at the Ricardo Richards Elementary School in my second and fourth grade classes who spent their lunch recess time teaching me all of the material found in this book. Without their enthusiasm and interest, I would never have been able to collect the live sound field recordings.

Steve Cash for his love, encouragement and enduring support throughout the development and completion of this book, and for understanding why it had to be written.

The Ellis family who gave me my education and my attitude without which I would never have had as much fun as I've had doing this book.

George Seaman for permission to use Cruzan definitions and proverbs taken from his books, "VIRGIN ISLANDS DICTIONARY" and "NOT SO CAT WALK" both available on St. Croix, Virgin Islands.

Carl Bernstein who helped me with the original music transcriptions and Barry Bell who took the photographs.

Michael Frank for Macintosh Desktop Publishing: graphic design, word processing and editing, artwork (hands!), music typesetting and page layout; this book was produced entirely on the Mac using: MacDraw, MacPaint, SuperPaint, Word, Finale, PageMaker, and Tricia's LaserWriter Plus.

Ilaria Arpino for the cover design and original artwork. Illustrations are based on sketches by "Champ".

Fred Weis for behind the scenes planning, support and enthusiasm.

Dennis Nardi of Strata Studio who mastered the cassette tape.

Tossi Aaron who started me in Orff-Shulwerk in 1970.

The Philadelphia Free Library for assistance with maps.

Judith Tucker at World Music Press for her help, support, advice, and enthusiasm.

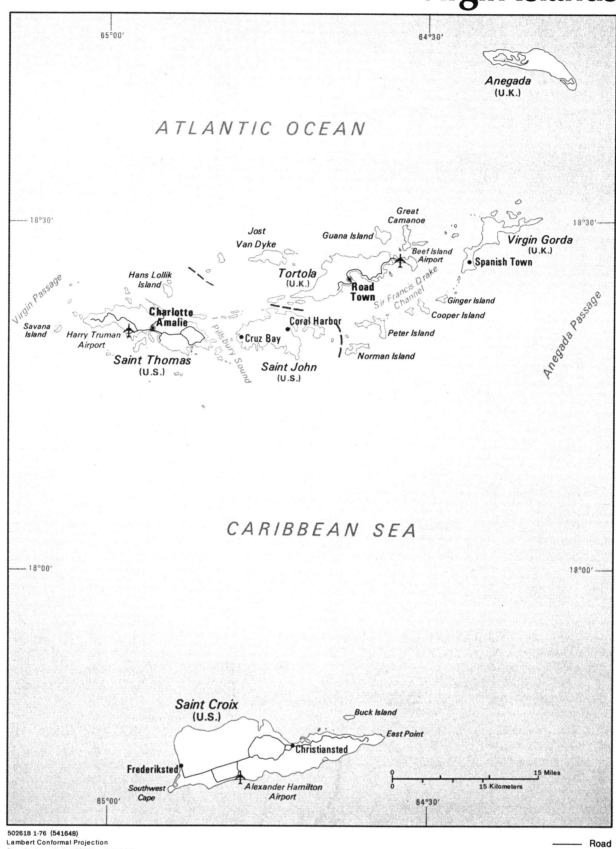

The Caribbean

Picture Page

Hands:

1. sky - ground

2. clap cross right

3. clap cross left

4. across shoulders

5. patchen

6. fish tail

7. clap partner

Legend

1. Clap Pattern_____

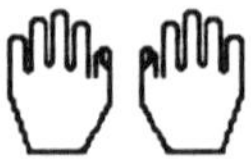

2. Foot Work_____

3. Hips_____

4. Circle Game_____

5. Line Dance_____

6. Call and Response_____

7. Jump Rope_____

Table of Contents

Foreword and Introduction ....*i*
Acknowledgements ....*xv*
Maps ....*xvi*
Picture Page ....*xviii*
Legend ....*xx*
Table of Contents ....*xxii*

Chapter 1
Clap Pattern: Spoken Chants and Songs

Domino 3
I Saw Your Boyfriend 4
Shame Shame Shame 5
Twenty-Four Black Birds 6
Jack Be Nimble 7
Four White Horses 8
Down Down Baby 10
Under the Blue Bush 12
The Number Song 13
Mama Lama 14
Mosquito One 15
Mayzoo 16
Humming Bird I 18
Humming Bird II 20
Una Dos y Tres 22
Coolie Man House 24
Grandmother 26
Have You Ever Seen a Chicken 28

Chapter 2
Circle Games, Line Dances, Call and Response

There's a Brown Girl in the Ring 31
Ding Dong 32
Kiss Kiss 33
Here Comes Jockey 34
Down in the River 36

Alabamba	37
Dutch Girl	38
Mother Goose	39
Miss Mary Had a Baby	40
In a Fine Castle	42
Santa Me Sayzee	43
Jane and Louisa	44
I Went to California	45
Bucket of Water	46
A Tisket A Tasket	48
Christmas Coming	49
Mister Wolf	50

Chapter 3
Jump Rope: Spoken Chants and Songs, Elimination Games and Jokes

Lambooshay	53
Teddy Bear	53
Johnny Jump on One Foot	54
I'm a Liar	54
Down by the Service Station	55
Solomon Agrundy	55
My Mother Your Mother	56
Cinderella	57
Down by the River	57
Sally Sally Water	58
All Together	58
The Queen of Hearts	59
Sea Shell Cockle Shell	60
Fish Fish	61
Elimination Games and Jokes	62
Glossary	64
Omissions	67
Further Reading	68

Chapter 1

Clap Pattern: Spoken Chants and Songs

AH BUDDY, ME A JIG BUT NO MOTION.
Isn't this magnificent? You are working like the devil but not getting anywhere.

DE LONGES' WAY ROUN' IS DE SHORTES' WAY HOME.
Here we have a version of the old adage, "the more haste the less speed". To take the time to do a thing right will pay off in the end.

MAN DON' BUY DOG TO SHOUT SELF.
Precisely. You never consciously indulge in acts that may backfire on you.

MAN DEAD, MAN DEY.
Implies that life will go on in spite of death. Might also have a waggish connotation: If a woman loses her man, there is always another to take his place.

Domino

Dom-i-no Dom-i-no Dom-i-no a bis-cuit ooh chee chee wah wah a bisc-uit.

How do you know my lov-er a bisc-uit he's so fine a bis-cuit

just like a cher-ry wine a bis-cuit. Dom-i-no Dom-i-no Dom-i-no a bis-cuit

ooh chee chee wah wah a bisc-uit.

ACTION

a b c c a b d d a b e e a b d d

a - clap partner sky-ground
b - clap partner REVERSE sky-ground
c - clap partner
d - point the thumb over the shoulder
e - clap own hands

-Roland

YO EYE 'FRAID WUK.
  You're sizing up the work before you start.

BUSH HA' EARS, LONG GRASS CARRY NEWS.
  This little proverb prompted, no doubt, by the almost mysterious way gossip, scandal and news could spread over the island. It might also be a warning to those with loose tongues.

I Saw Your Boyfriend

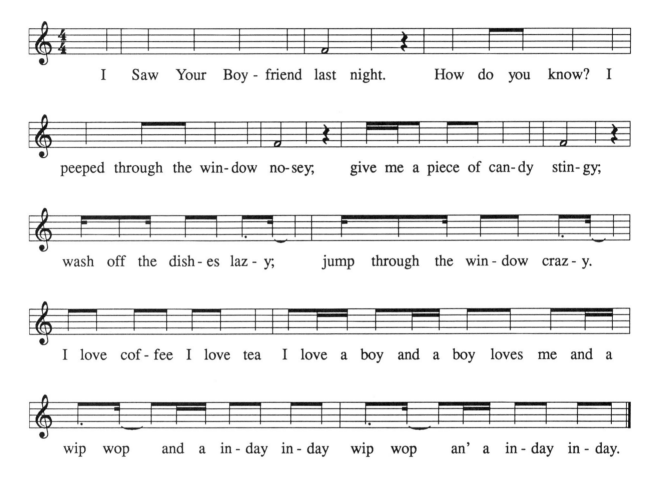

I Saw Your Boy-friend last night. How do you know? I peeped through the win-dow no-sey; give me a piece of can-dy stin-gy; wash off the dish-es laz-y; jump through the win-dow craz-y. I love cof-fee I love tea I love a boy and a boy loves me and a wip wop and a in-day in-day wip wop an' a in-day in-day.

ACTION

a b c d c e c d c f g h h f g h h

* play until first "wip wop" starts.

a - clap partner (sky ground)
b - clap partner
c - clap own hands
d - clap partner cross right
e - clap partner cross left
f - put hands on hips and swing them to the right
g - then move hips to the left
h - thrust the pelvis forward and move them back to the center again

Shame Shame Shame

Shame Shame Shame; I don't want to go to Mex-i-co no more more more; there's a

big fat po-lice-man at the door door door; if I hold him by his col-lar, oh

Lord he will hol-ler; I don't want to go to Mex-i-co no more more more;

shame shame shame.

ACTION

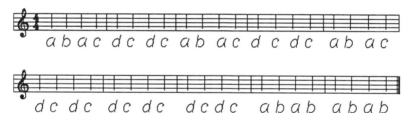

a - fish tail left
b - fish tail right
c - cross right, grab partner's hand and pull it down, then let go
d - cross left, grab partner's hand and pull it down, then let go

WHEN T'IEF T'IEF FROM T'IEF MASSA GOD LAUGH.
*A striking observation clothed in provocative humor.
How else? If a thief steals from another thief, surely
God must laugh, – as all the rest of us will.*

Twenty-Four Black Birds

Twen-ty Four Black Birds in the air Oy Pa-pa shoot them by the pair Oy

Ma-ma fry them in the pan Oy Pa-pa eat them like a man Oy

when Pa-pa done he lick he hand Oy Ma-ma say Pa-pa is a greed-y man Oy

Pa-pa say Ma-ma don't talk so loud Oy there are chil-dren in the yard Oy

la la la la la   la la la   la la la la la   la la la   la la la la la   la la la

la la la la la la la Oy.

ACTION

a b a b c

a - clap own hands
b - clap partner
c - this is the 'la la' verse; all players dance wherever and however they please.

WHEN PUSSY BELLY FULL HE SAY RATTA STINK.
A rich man often forgets the days of his poverty.

Jack Be Nimble

Jack Be Nim-ble Jack be quick; Jack jump o-ver the can-dle stick; all a-

round the lim-be-rack, he can do the lim-be-rack; my moth-er

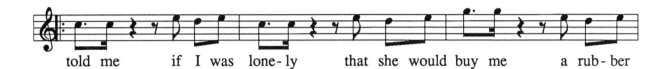

told me if I was lone-ly that she would buy me a rub-ber

dol-ly; my sis-ter

3rd Verse: My sister told me if I was lonely that she would buy me a rubber ducky;
4th Verse: My auntie told me if I was lonely that she would buy me a sexy panty;
5th Verse: My father told me if I was lonely that he would carry me to New York City.

ACTION

a b c d   c e c c   f b c d   c e c c

a - clap partner sky-ground
b - clap partner
c - clap own hands
d - clap cross right
e - clap cross left
f - clap back of hands

IF YO' PUT YO' EAR A MANGO ROOT YO' WILL HEAR CRAB COUGH.

One of the beautiful ones. Can't you just see someone down on his knees by a mango root listening? If you have patience and listen that close, you are bound to learn things.

Four White Horses

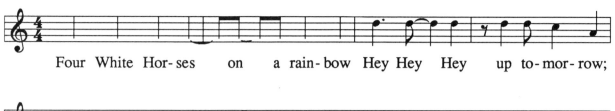

ACTION

Four children form a circle and join hands:

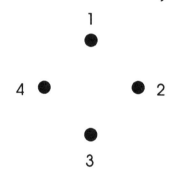

TODAY FO' YO', TOMORROW FO' ME.
 This is the "every dog has his day" theme.

WHA GOAT EAT THE KIDS SUCK.
 The nourishment of the parents, (background, etc.) becomes the inheritance of the offspring. A man is the product of his upbringing.

a - the children in the circle join hands and gently swing them back and forth
b - clap own hands
c - clap partner - children (1+2) together and (3+4) together

d - the reverse of '*c*'

e - clap partner - children (1+3) clap up high in the air while children (2+4) clap low under (1+3)

f - the reverse of '*e*'

Down Down Baby

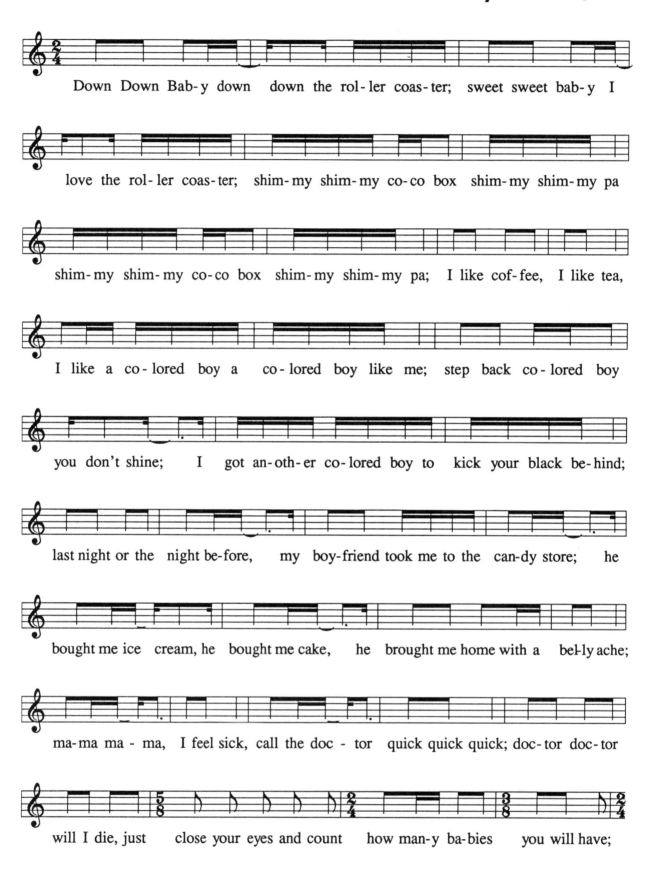

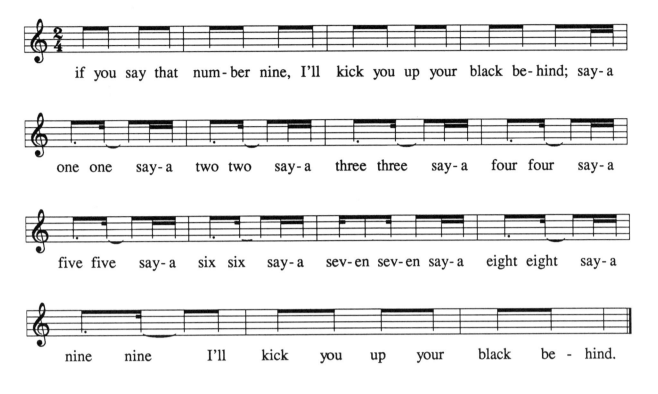

ACTION

a - clap sky-ground
b - clap partner hands
c - clap own hands
d - clap cross right
e - clap cross left

NIGHT DANGER, MORNIN' COMPLAIN.
   Girl gets pregnant at night, complains in the morning!
   No use to complain after the danger is past.

WHA' YO' DIDN' WAN' TO SEE, YO' NOW HAB IN YO' HAN'.
   Yes, babies have a way of coming!

Under the Blue Bush

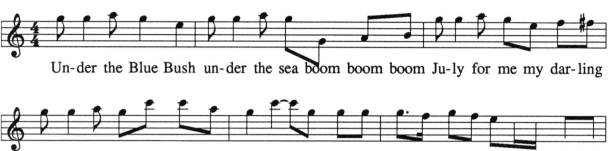

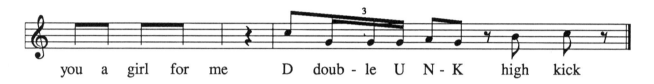

ACTION

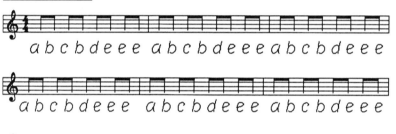

a - clap partner sky-ground
b - clap own hands
c - clap cross right
d - clap cross left
e - clap partner
f - hands on hips and jump then...
g - kick one leg high in the air

LIZZARD LAY EGG, BUT HIM NO FOWL.
An astute piece of natural history, quite clearly meaning: do not be taken in by apparently similar events or things— they may be significantly different.

The Number Song

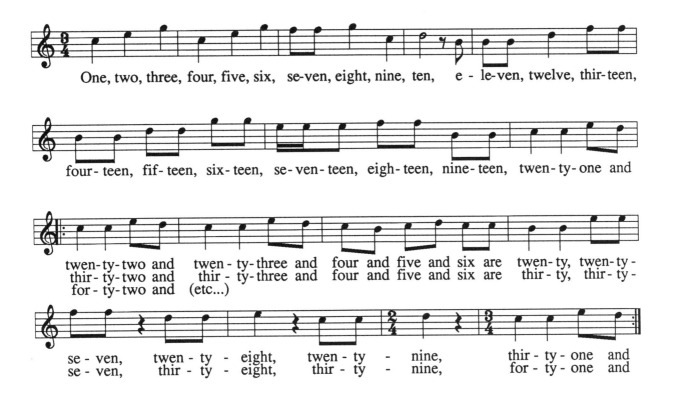

One, two, three, four, five, six, se-ven, eight, nine, ten, e-le-ven, twelve, thir-teen, four-teen, fif-teen, six-teen, se-ven-teen, eigh-teen, nine-teen, twen-ty-one and

twen-ty-two and twen-ty-three and four and five and six are twen-ty, twen-ty-se-ven, twen-ty-eight, twen-ty-nine, thir-ty-one and
thir-ty-two and thir-ty-three and four and five and six are thir-ty, thir-ty-se-ven, thir-ty-eight, thir-ty-nine, for-ty-one and
for-ty-two and (etc...)

Continue to one hundred

NOT SO CAT WALK DEY DOES MOUSE.
   Don't judge a book by its cover. The sleepy-looking cat can pounce into life in a minute.

CANE NO GROW LIKE GRASS.
   If you think something is going to be easy, better take another look. It may be more difficult than you expected.

EASY TIE TIGER, HARD MEK BABOON BLOW SHELL.
   The blowing of conch shells often denoted trouble. If you pushed a man too hard he might just "blow" the shell on you.

HAN'SOME FACE 'OMAN IS NOT DE BESTES OF 'OMAN.
   Do not be misguided by a pretty face.

LAS' RATTA IN DE HOLE LEAVE HE TAIL OUT.
   If you are last you may get caught.

Mama Lama

Ma - ma La - ma Cu - ma la - ma ma - ma la - ma piz - za

Ma-ma La-ma Cu-ma la-ma ma-ma la-ma piz-za Oh no no no no la piz-za

Oh no no no no la piz-za ee-nie mee-nie dix-a pee-nie Ooh va da ooh ba nee nee

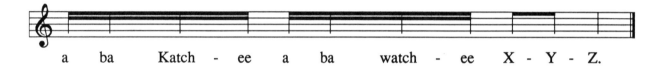
a ba Katch - ee a ba watch - ee X - Y - Z.

ACTION

To prepare: extend the left hand diagonally to be ready to meet the right hand after the hip has been slapped

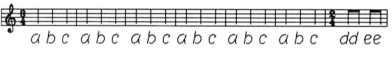
a b c a b c a b c a b c a b c a b c dd ee

dd ee dd ee dd ee fg fh fg fh fg fh fg fh

a - slap own right hip
b - simultaneously bring the right hand to slap your own left hand while partners hit the backs of their left hands together. Keep in mind that this motion is going left like a baseball bat
c - hands are still in fish tail position and partners now hit the backs of their right hands going right
d - keep the backs of left hands touching and then clap own hands
e - hit backs of left hands together in fish tail position
f - clap own hand
g - partners keep backs of left hands touching while their right hands clap up above
h - same as g but clap down below

Mosquito One

Mos-qui-to One mos-qui-to two mos-qui-to jump in the old man's shoe;

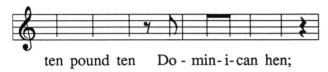
ten pound ten Do-min-i-can hen;

(1)
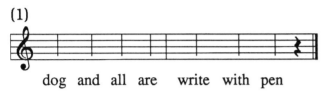
dog and all are write with pen

(2)

mon-key jump up and jump out a-gain.

ACTION

clap pattern:

a   b   c   d   e   d   f   d

foot pattern:
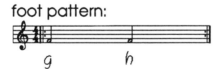
g   h

a - slap partner arms straight 'give me five'
b - reverse of a
c - clap partner
d - clap own hands
e - clap cross right
f - clap cross left
g - right heel forward
h - left heel forward

Mayzoo

YO' A SPOONER BILL, YO' A CUT TWO SIDE.
  This was a sugar cane bill which could cut on both sides, hence it represented one of ambiguous thinking. One who plays both sides.

WHEN MONKEY COME A LOW LAN' HARDSHIP DEY A MOUNTAIN
  When times are hard people will move around more and often indulge in unaccustomed pursuits.
  Necessity dictates change.

BETTAH BELLY BUS' DAN GOOD T'ING WASTE.
  Take advantage of good times, they may not come again.

ACTION

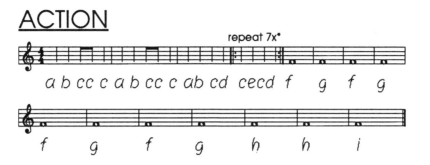

*repeat until measure 11: 'A- B- C- D-'

a - clap partner sky-ground
b - clap partner
c - clap own hands
d - clap cross right
e - clap cross left
f - partners stand with left hand on hip while the right
    index finger is pointing towards the right ear
    and rotates in a small circle
g - total reverse of f
h - partners slide the sides of their skirts up their thighs
i - all players freeze until someone moves and then
    the game starts over

WE SAY "MORNING", BUT WE DON' KNOW WHEY NIGHT GOIN MEET US.

A nice thought and very well put. The destiny of each day begins in the morning. Who knows what will be by sunset?

LITTLE AX CUT DOWN BIG TREE.

A man may be small, but accomplish big things.

IF YO' NO LIB IN A HOUSE, YO' NO KNOW DE LEAK.

You have to wear the shoe to know the pinch. How can the man on the horse know the troubles of the man with the hoe?

Humming Bird I

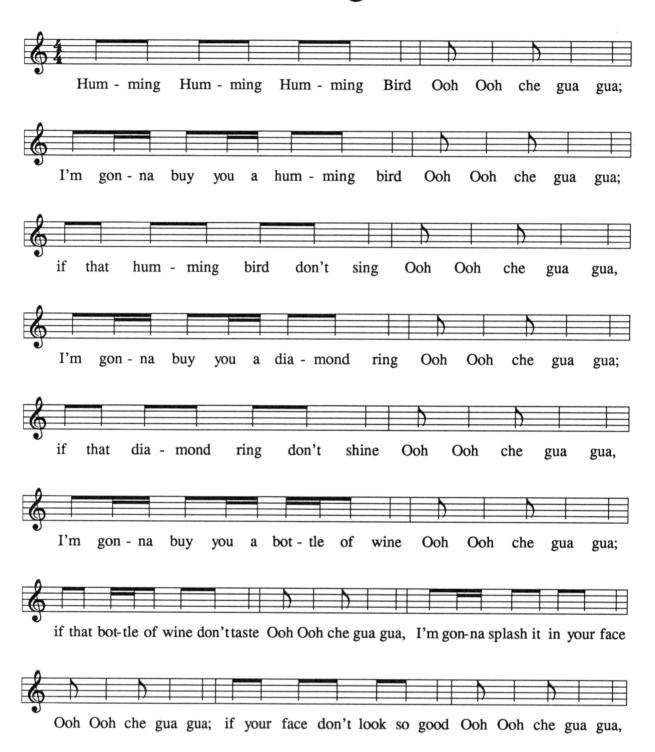

I'm gon-na tell the neigh-bor-hood Ooh Ooh che gua gua Ooh Ooh che gua gua

Ooh   Ooh   che   gua   gua.

ACTION

aa aa   bb bb bb bb   aa aa   c c c c c c c c

a - clasp hands with fingers interlaced and turn
      the palms facing outward <u>then</u> clap your partner
b - rub hands up and down one side of your hip
c - rub the other side of your hip

KILL MAMMY GIVE PICKNY, PICKNY EAT;
BUT KILL PICKNY AN' GIVE MAMMY, MAMMY NO EAT.
   This is the old story of mother love. The child may betray the
   mother, but never the mother the child.

Humming Bird II

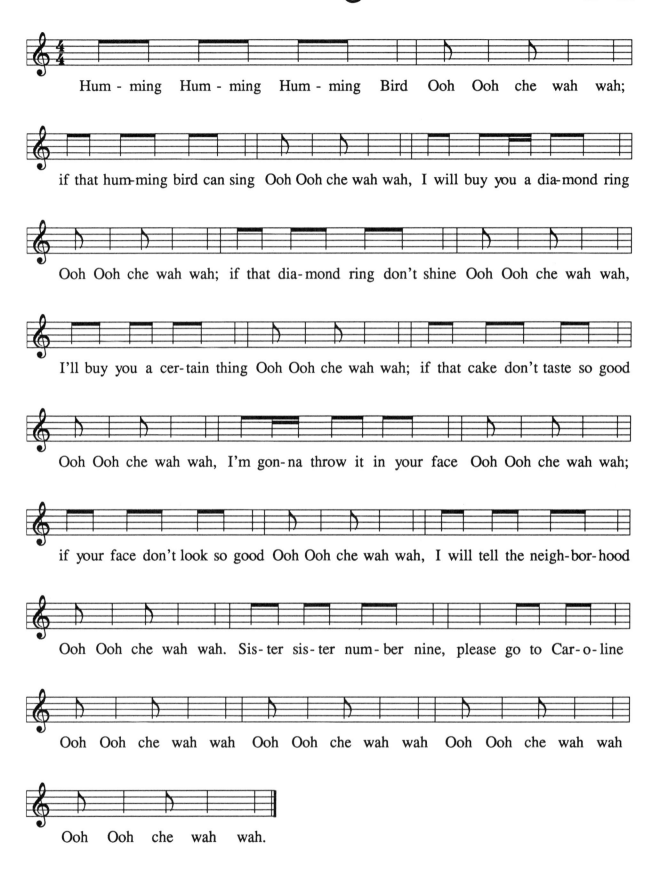

ACTION

aaaa bb bbbb bb aaaa cc cc cc cc aaaa

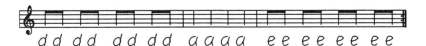
dd dd dd dd aaaa ee ee ee ee

a - clasp hands with fingers interlaced and turn the palms facing outward <u>then</u> clap your partner
b - break the clasp and rub your own face with your hands
c - with fingers interlaced, rub your own belly up and down
d - child 'A' will rub child 'B's face while child 'B' rubs 'A's belly
e - the reverse of d

It is interesting to watch the kids alternate between rubbing themselves to rubbing their partner's face while getting their belly rubbed. This can be most beneficial for the emotionally or learning disabled child. This game promotes spatial and body awareness, timing, and stimulates trust.

HARD WORDS BRUK NO BONES.
Who cares about hard words when you are still in one piece.
Better a scolding than a licking.

IF YO' PLAY WID DOG (PUPPY) HE LICK YO' MOUT'.
This is one of the best known of the local proverbs.
It means that "familiarity breeds contempt."

Una Dos y Tres

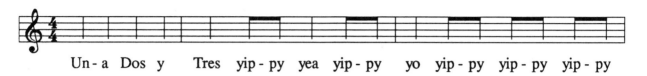
Un-a Dos y Tres yip-py yea yip-py yo yip-py yip-py yip-py

yea you got-ta in you got-ta out you got-ta cha cha cha you got-ta in you got-ta

out you got - ta cha cha cha

ACTION

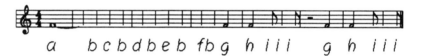
a b c b d b e b f b g h i i i   g h i i i

Four children form a circle and join hands:

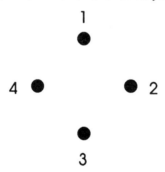

YO' CAN PROMISE YO' BACK, BUT YO' CAN' PROMISE YO' BELLY.
   You might put off buying a suit of clothes, but you wouldn't want to forego eating. Are dreams not pretty hollow things on an empty stomach?

CONGO SAW WUSS DAN OBEAH.
   I am told that this means that ungratefulness is worse than witchcraft.

a - the children in the circle join hands and gently swing them back and forth
b - clap own hands
c - clap partner - children (1+2) together and (3+4) together

d - the reverse of 'c'

e - clap partner - children (1+3) clap up high in the air while children (2+4) clap low under (1+3)
f - the reverse of 'f'

g - everyone jumps forward towards the middle
h - everyone jumps back out again
i - on 'cha cha cha', all children jump to the right then left then back to their original places

Coolie Man House

24

down Ka - low - chee Ka - low - chee Ka - low - chee come

up a - hi - ka a - hi - ka a - hi - ka and out the fi - re down there.

ACTION

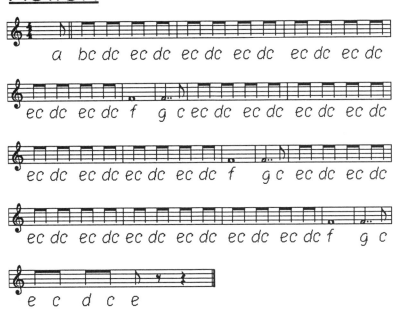

a - clap partner wrists crossed
b - clap partner
c - clap own hands
d - clap partner cross right
e - clap partner cross left
f - shimmy the hips moving down to the floor
g - shimmy the hips moving up to position

PIG SAY, "MAMMY WHA' MEK YO' MOUT' LONG SO?"
SHE SAY, "WAIT PICKNY YO' WILL SEE."
Age and experience reveal many things youth doesn't know.

Grandmother

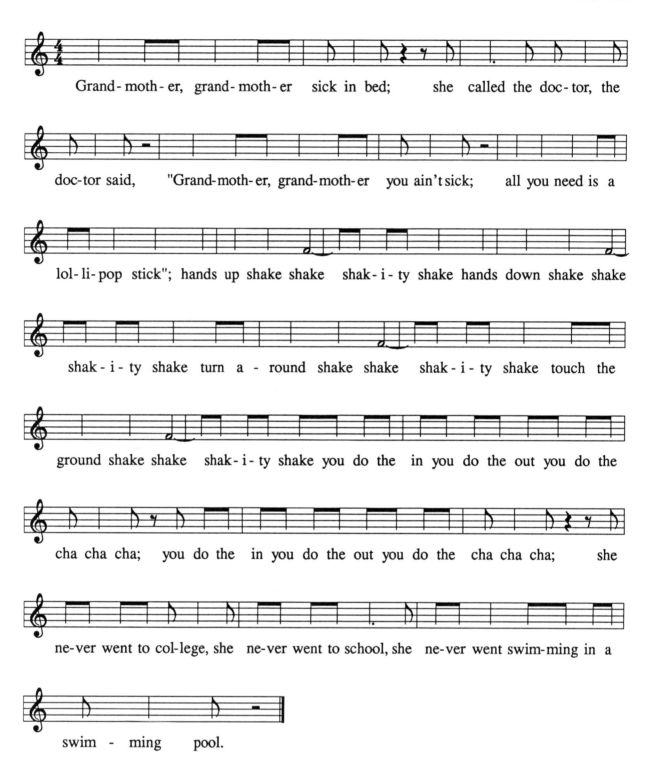

Grand-moth-er, grand-moth-er sick in bed; she called the doc-tor, the doc-tor said, "Grand-moth-er, grand-moth-er you ain't sick; all you need is a lol-li-pop stick"; hands up shake shake shak-i-ty shake hands down shake shake shak-i-ty shake turn a-round shake shake shak-i-ty shake touch the ground shake shake shak-i-ty shake you do the in you do the out you do the cha cha cha; you do the in you do the out you do the cha cha cha; she ne-ver went to col-lege, she ne-ver went to school, she ne-ver went swim-ming in a swim-ming pool.

SMOKE YO' CIGAR BUT MIN' HOW YO' SPIT.
Be careful you don't get in water that's too deep for you.

26

ACTION

To prepare: extend the left hand diagonally to be ready to meet the right hand after the hip has been slapped

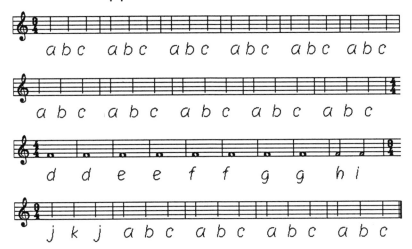

a - slap own right hip
b - simultaneously bring the right hand to slap your own left while partners slap the backs of their left hands
c - hands are still in a prayer position and partners now hit the backs of their right hands going right
d - raise arms high and shake the hands around
e - lower arms and shake hands around
f - turn around 360° shaking the hands
g - touch the ground and continue shaking the hands
h - jump forward toward your partner
i - jump back out again
j - jump sideways to the right
k - jump left to the other side

WHEN PLANTAIN TREE WANT DEAD HE BEAR.
This represents the cycle of life. Old age is often a fruitful period.

WHEN YO' A DIG GRAVE DIG TWO.
Excellent. Beware when making plans, you may be planning for yourself!

Have You Ever Seen a Chicken

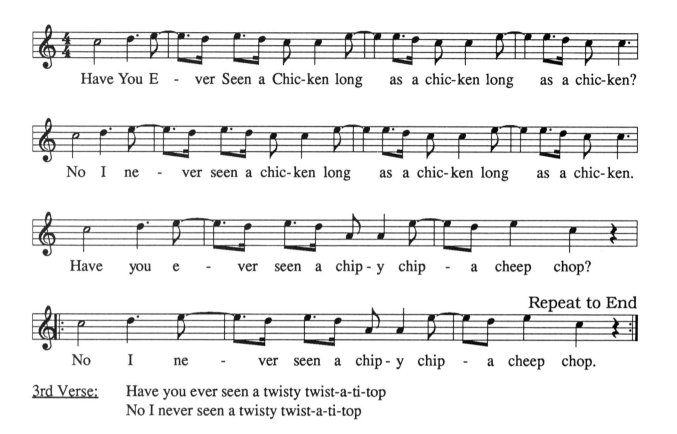

3rd Verse: Have you ever seen a twisty twist-a-ti-top
No I never seen a twisty twist-a-ti-top

ACTION

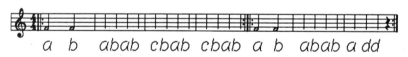

a b abab cbab cbab a b abab a dd

a b a b a b a e e

a - clap partner
b - clap own hands
c - spread the hands far apart on 'long'
d - make a chopping motion on the inside of the left elbow
e - shake the hips from side to side

WHEN NAGUR SAY, 'DAT FOWL FAT,' HE GOIN' T'IEF UM DE SAME NIGHT FO' HE PICKNY SUPPER.

Beware the person eyeing and praising your goods; he may be contemplating relieving you of them.

Chapter 2

Circle Games
Line Dances
Call and Response

DE LONGES' LIVER SEE DE MOS'.
　　　Time will tell. Age has its rewards. One of the compensations
　　　of age is to know and have seen much.

EASY DOG BITE HARD.
　　　Beware of an easy-going person; they may
　　　have a bad temper when aroused.

WHA' EYE DON' SEE HEART DON' GRIEVE FO'.
　　　You can't feel bad about something you don't
　　　see or know about.

There's a Brown Girl in the Ring

3rd Verse: Pick out your partner tra la la la la
pick out your partner tra la la la la la la
pick out your partner tra la la la la
and she looks like a sugar and a plum plum plum

ACTION

1st Verse: children form a circle, join hands, and walk around the child in the center

2nd Verse: the child in the center makes up some motion

3rd Verse: the center child takes another child from the circle and they exchange places while the outer circle keeps moving

This song is one of the most widely known and popular in the Caribbean.

31

Ding Dong

Ding Dong my dar-ling, my su-gar plum, my sweet-heart, which one would you

rath - er, ice - cream or cake?

ACTION

This is a simple song the children sing together while standing in a circle.

MASSA BULL, MASSA COW.
    An old and well known saying. In other words, everything on the estate belonged to the "Massa" or owner. All amounts to the same thing.

SLEEP HAB NO MASSA
    A deep and beautiful reflection. It expresses the sovereignty of sleep.

"PLEASE" AM A GOOD DOG AN' HE KEEP DON' COS' NUTTIN.
    It doesn't cost anything to be polite.

STONE A WATAH NO KNOW WHEN SUN HOT.
    The sheltered person is often unaware of reality.

Kiss Kiss

(G)

Down on the car-pet I go like a black girl in the air;
rise and stand up on your knees and kiss the one that you love the best;
when I'm mar-ried, I'll give you joy, first a boy, and sec-ond a girl;
he this boy, she this girl, Kiss Kiss and say 'good-bye.'

ACTION

Children form a circle, hold hands, and walk around the center child. The circle walks during the entire song.

a - the center child kneels on the ground
b - the center child stands up
c - the center child kisses someone
d - the center child sings along with the group
e - on 'kiss kiss,' the center child kisses the same child twice more

EASY BULL WALK FAR.
How true. Quietly plodding can take one far.

Here Comes Jockey

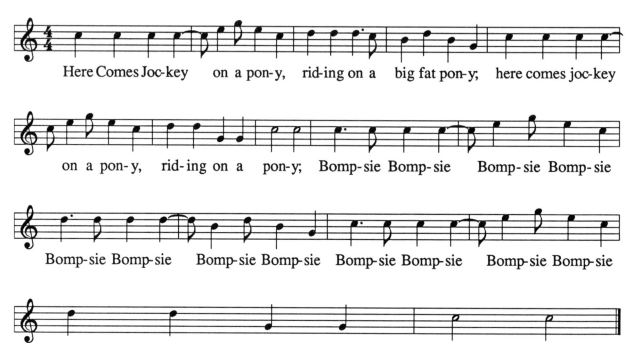

CAT GOT BONE A PLAY WID, DOG WANT UM.
   Here we see the same inference to wealth and poverty.
   The one has too much; the other not enough.

BEFO' FACE AN' BEHIN' BACK NO DE SAME T'ING.
   What you might do and say behind a person's back
   you might not attempt to their face.

FULL BELLY TELL EMPTY BELLY KEEP HEART.
   How easy it is for the prosperous to tell the poor
   have courage and work hard. The age-old story of
   those who have and those who have not.

**DRUNK MAN TELL LAMP POST,
"ASK PARDON, SAH."**
   Beware the evils of alcohol. Under its influence,
   you may even ask pardon of a lamp post!

ACTION

a - the leader skips around the inside of the circle while the circle claps the steady beat
b - the leader stops in front of someone and they start to hop in place while alternating left and right kicking motions. This is called a Blaking Step.
c - these children exchange places and the new leader skips around the circle; now the song starts over again.

d - when everyone sings the 'bompsie' chorus, the leader will pick someone; they will link arms, and swing each other around the center of the circle
e - they both trot around the center and both pick a new partner. This is how you get more jockeys into the game. Now the game starts over again

WHA' GO OVER A HOSS BACK GO UNDER HE BELLY.
In the old days the horse was a symbol of status. All the big people rode horses. The above proverb warns against hautiness. What's on the horse's back can someday be under its belly.

Down in the River

ACTION

Children form a circle and one child kneels down in the center pretending to water the grass and flowers. The outside circle hold hands and gently swing them back and forth while walking around.

NO TEK SHAME SHAKE HAN' WID COCOBAY NAGUR.
Do not allow sympathy to get the better of your judgement.

Alabamba

ACTION

The children form a circle and hold hands as they sing the song. Each child gets a number and when it is called, they go to the center and dance.

BUCKRA LUB IS COCOBAY LUB.
Beware the white man's love for you. It is not a good love. Accept it with reservation.

HUNGRY CHIGGERS NO RESPEC' DE WHITE FOOT OF BUCKRA LADY.
A satirical gem. Just picture the "Buckra lady" with a foot full of chiggers!

SO LONG WOMAN A BREED WAR NEBAH DONE.
An ominous prediction garbed in an ancient truth.

Dutch Girl

I'm a lit-tle Dutch Girl, Dutch girl, Dutch girl; I'm a lit-tle Ditch girl, Dutch girl now.

Additional verses are sung alternately by the boys or girls:

2nd Verse: I'm a little Dutch boy, Dutch boy, Dutch boy
I'm a little Dutch boy, Dutch boy now (today).

3rd Verse: Go away I hate you, I hate you, I hate you
Go away I hate you, I hate you now

4th Verse: Oh why do you hate me, you hate me, you hate me
Oh why do you hate me, you hate me now

5th Verse: Because you stole my apron, my apron, my apron
Because you stole my apron, my apron now

6th Verse: Oh will you please forgive me, forgive me, forgive me
Oh will you please forgive me, forgive me now

7th Verse: Oh yes I will forgive you, forgive you, forgive you
Oh yes I will forgive you, forgive you now

8th Verse: Oh let us go to London, to London, to London
Oh let us go to London, to London now

ACTION

the boys and girls face each other in two lines

1 - girls curtsy every third beat
2 - boys bow every third beat
3 - girls shoo boys away with their hands and the boys walk backward
4 - boys walk forward singing
5 - girls cross arms on their chest then patchen and repeat
6 - the boy bends down on one knee
7 - partners switch positions
8 - partners hook the inside arms and swing around while skipping

ANY BELLYFUL A ONE BELLYFUL.
   Help is help, do not question the source.

Mother Goose

C+R

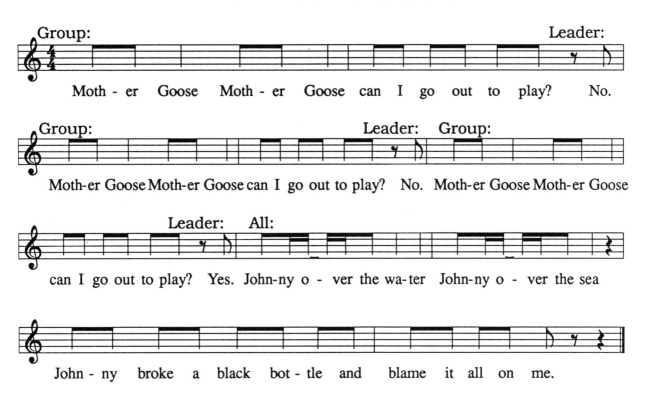

The leader stands in front of everyone at a distance and faces them, speaking in a loud, booming voice; children respond in sassy voices:

Leader:	'Children, children where have you been?'
Response:	'To Grandpa-pa.'
L:	'What did he give you?'
R:	'Bread and cheese.'
L:	'Where is mine?'
R:	'On top of the shelf.'
L:	'How can I reach it?'
R:	'On a broken chair.'
L:	'Suppose I fall.'
R:	'I don't care.'
L:	'Where's your manners?'
R:	'In my shoe.'
L:	'Who is the dirty stinkin' dog?'
R:	'You.'
L:	'Come look-a nearer.'
R:	'Look me-a.' [here]
L:	'Come look-a nearer.'
R:	'Look me-a.'
L:	'Nearer still.'
R:	'Look me-a.
L:	'Nearer still.'

Leader runs after and tries to tag each player. The last one tagged is the next leader and the chant begins again.

ACTION

a - clap neighbor
b - rotate arm in a circle

The children form a circle. They rotate their arms backwards and come up to clap their neighbor's hands. It is interesting to note that the song ends with the rhythm of the merengue.

** Alternate music at measures 14, 15, and 16:

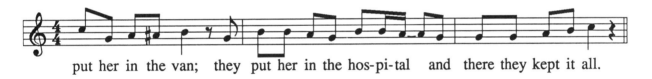

put her in the van; they put her in the hos-pi-tal and there they kept it all.

LAS' PICKNY KILL MAMMY.
You may overcome many problems, but sometimes the last will get you.

IF YO' NO HEAR "TEK CARE" YO' WILL HEAR "WHA' MATTER?"
An admonition to those who refuse to listen, and only do so after they are hurt.

A PINT A HELP BETTAH DAN A TOUSAN' PITIES.
A little help at a time of need is preferable to a generous pity.

In a Fine Castle

C+R

All: In a Fine Cas-tle do you hear my Sis-sy-O, in a fine cas-tle do you hear my Sis-sy-O;

A: we want one of them do you hear my Sis-sy-O;

B: which one do you want do you hear my Sis-sy-O,

A: we want Mich-elle do you hear my Sis-sy-O;

B: what will you give her do you hear my Sis-sy-O,

A: we'll give her rot-ten eggs do you hear my Sis-sy-O;

B: that will suit her do you hear my Sis-sy-O;

A: we'll give her a gol-den ring do you hear my Sis-sy-O;

B: that will suit her do you hear my Sis-sy-O;

All: fare-well Mich-elle, go and get your gol-den ring.

ACTION

The children form two circles - groups A and B. This is a great call and response song. The kids hold hands and swing their arms back and forth through the whole song. In the fourth verse, group A chooses someone from group B and sings their name. In the last verse this child leaves group B and walks over to join group A. Now the game starts over and this time someone from group A will go over to group B.

Santa Me Sayzee

San-ta Me Say-zee, San-ta me say-zee, San-ta me say-zee all day long;

here comes Su-sie, Su - sie, Su-sie, Su-sie, here comes Su-sie all day long;

here comes an-oth-er one just like Su-sie, Su - sie, Su-sie, Su-sie all day long.

ACTION

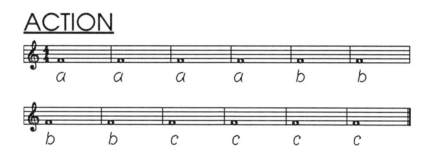

a a a a b b
b b c c c c

a - the partners hold hands and move them back and forth

b - one partner at the end of the line walks down the middle of the rows performing some movement

c - now her partner travels down the middle of the rows imitating the same movement as she pretends to be a twin

NO HANG YO' COTACOO WHEY YO' CAN' REACH UM.
   Don't aim higher than you are capable of reaching.

RIPE QUICK, ROTTEN QUICKER.
   Forcing something to mature before its time can destroy its usefulness.

Jane and Louisa

Jane and Lou-i-sa will soon come home dar-ling, soon come home dar-ling, soon come

home; Jane and Lou-i-sa will soon come home, in-to the beaut-i-ful gar-den.

<u>2nd Verse:</u> How would you like me to pick a rose darling,
Pick a rose darling, pick a rose;
How would you like me to pick a rose,
Into the beautiful garden.

<u>3rd Verse:</u> How would you like me to dance with you..., etc.

<u>4th Verse:</u> Would you all like me to kiss with you..., etc.

ACTION

<u>1st Verse:</u> The boys and girls face each other in two lines and they both sing

<u>2nd Verse:</u> The boys sing while they bend down and pretend to pick a rose and give it to the girl opposite them. The girls can help sing if they like

<u>3rd Verse:</u> The boys sing while they take their partner and dance with them. Again, girls may sing if they like

<u>4th Verse:</u> Now the children kiss each other on the cheek every time they sing the word 'kiss.' This verse is always exciting for everyone.

I Went to California

I went to Cal-i-for-nia far far a-way; I met a sen-or-i-ta with flow-ers in her hair OH shake it shake it shake it shake it if you can and if you can not shake it you do the best you can OH rub it to the bot-tom rub it to the top and turn a-round and turn a-round un-til you make a stop.

ACTION

Form a circle with a child in the middle.

a - clap own hands
b - everyone moves the hips from side to side (<u>once</u> each beat)
c - shake the hips quickly while stooping to the floor and coming back up
d - while the circle claps the steady beat, the center child covers her eyes and turns around pointing outward. On the word <u>stop</u>, the center child exchanges places with the circle child and the game starts over.

Bucket of Water

Draw me a Buc-ket of Wa-ter for my ol-dest daugh-ter, none in the bunch and four out the bunch you go un-der sis-ter Sal-ly.

2nd Verse: Draw me a bucket of water / for my oldest daughter you got / three in the bunch and one out the bunch / you go under sister Sally.

3rd Verse: Draw me a bucket of water / for my oldest daughter you got / two in the bunch and two out the bunch / you go under sister Sally.

4th Verse: Draw me a bucket of water / for my oldest daughter you got / one in the bunch and three out the bunch / you go under sister Sally.

5th Verse:

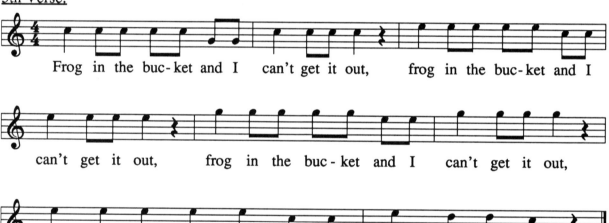

Frog in the buc-ket and I can't get it out, frog in the buc-ket and I can't get it out, frog in the buc-ket and I can't get it out, frog in the buc-ket and I can't get it out.

IF WIN' NO BLOW YO' NO SEE FOWL BOTTOM.
In other words, it's really an "ill-wind" that does do some good.

MAN GOT TWO WIFE HIM SLEEP HUNGRY.
It's possible that there can be too much of a good thing.

ACTION

```
      1
      ●

4 ●       ● 2

      ●
      3
```

<u>1st Verse:</u>   Four children are in a group; (1+3) hold hands and pull back and forth alternating left and right <u>under</u> (2+4) who are doing the same

<u>2nd Verse:</u>   The same action occurs until they sing 'you go under sister Sally'. Then (1+3) pick up their arms over girl #2 who is now in the bunch

<u>3rd Verse:</u>   same as 2nd verse only (1+3) pick up their arms over girl #4 while (2+4) keep going

<u>4th Verse:</u>   same as 3rd verse only (4+2) pick up their arms over girl #1

<u>5th Verse:</u>   on 'Frog', children clap their hands and kick their feet any way they like until the end of the song.

ANY DIRTY WATAH COOL COPPER.
   In a pinch anything will do. Can we read into this a not so subtle sexual connotation?

EBERY DAY BUCKET GO A WELL, ONE DAY DE BUCKET WILL STOP DEY.
   If you use anything unwisely, one day it will come to an end.

A Tisket A Tasket

A Tis-ket A Tas-ket a green and yel-low bas-ket; I

wrote a let-ter to my mom and on the way I drop it T-I-M-E time to drop it

T-I-M-E time to drop it T-I-M-E time to drop it.

ACTION

Children form a circle and swing their arms in and out. The leader carries a stick and skips behind everyone in the circle. When 'I drop it' is sung, the leader drops the stick behind someone who picks it up and chases him. The leader tries to go around the circle and get into the other child's space before being tagged while the chant, 'T- I- M- E time to drop it' is continually spoken.

**RATTA SAY HE NO MIN' DE MAN WHA' KILL UM,
HE MIN' DE MAN DAT SAY "SEE UM DEY."**
Save your condemnation for the betrayer rather than the executioner. A certainly delightful and astute manipulation of subtle moral principals.

Christmas Coming

Ma-ma make a john-ny cake Christ-mas Com-ing; ma-ma make a john-ny cake

Christ-mas Com-ing; gua-va ber-ry, Christ-mas cher-ry.

ACTION

Stand in a circle and clap on all four beats.

DEBIL TEMPT, BUT HE NO FO'CE.
A real little beauty. The devil may point the way, but you don't have to follow the path.

GOOD FRIEN' BETTAH DAN MONKEY-WIDE POCKET.
How true. A good friend is worth more than gold.

EBERY PARSON CHRISTEN HE OWN CHILE FUS.
Blood is thicker than water. You look after your own.

"IF I BEEN KNOW," NEBAH COME FUS.
"Had I known," is a very poor excuse for anything

Mister Wolf

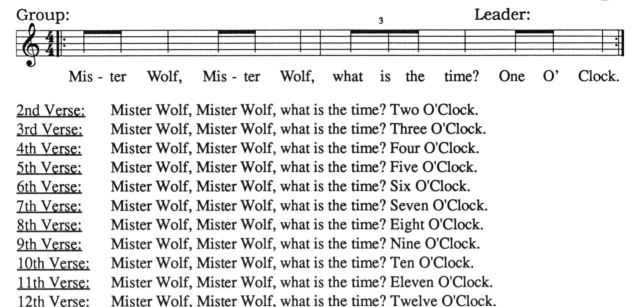

2nd Verse: Mister Wolf, Mister Wolf, what is the time? Two O'Clock.
3rd Verse: Mister Wolf, Mister Wolf, what is the time? Three O'Clock.
4th Verse: Mister Wolf, Mister Wolf, what is the time? Four O'Clock.
5th Verse: Mister Wolf, Mister Wolf, what is the time? Five O'Clock.
6th Verse: Mister Wolf, Mister Wolf, what is the time? Six O'Clock.
7th Verse: Mister Wolf, Mister Wolf, what is the time? Seven O'Clock.
8th Verse: Mister Wolf, Mister Wolf, what is the time? Eight O'Clock.
9th Verse: Mister Wolf, Mister Wolf, what is the time? Nine O'Clock.
10th Verse: Mister Wolf, Mister Wolf, what is the time? Ten O'Clock.
11th Verse: Mister Wolf, Mister Wolf, what is the time? Eleven O'Clock.
12th Verse: Mister Wolf, Mister Wolf, what is the time? Twelve O'Clock.

ACTION

The group gets louder and walks a little closer to the leader during each verse. When the leader says "Twelve O'Clock," he runs after the group and tries to tag someone while they are running away. The person who is tagged becomes the next leader when the game starts over.

WHEN BULLDOG SICK PUPPY BRITCHES FIT UM.
When real authority falters lesser souls will try to take over.

BETTAH FO' RIDE AN ASS WHA' CARRY YO' DAN A HOSS WHA' T'ROW YO'.
It is better to be contented with small things than to get in trouble reaching after those you can't afford.

GOOD MANAGEMENT BETTAH DAN BIG WAGES.
This could be interpreted to mean: It's not what you make but what you save that counts.

Chapter 3

Jump Rope: Spoken Chants and Songs
Elimination Games and Jokes

WHA' DON' MEET YO' DON' PASS YO'.
   Don't cross any bridges before you come to them.

WHO NO KNOW YO' CALL YO' "YOU".
   In the old days the proprieties of address were very strictly adhered to. This was a way of saying ignorance breeds impudence.

COCKROACHY SAY ONLY ONE LITTLE PLACE UNDER HE ARM STINK.
   Isn't this terrific? In other words, a person can't be all bad.

Lambooshay

Lam-boo-shay o - hi- o-lee- o lam-boo-shay o - lee-o-low see the far-mer ring
tie up the ex-tra string do re mi fa so la do ti do ta

END

lam - boo - shay o - hi - o - lee - o

- Lisa O'Neil

ACTION

* - at this point in the song, the rope is turned in one complete circle high above the jumper's head in one count.

Teddy Bear

Ted-dy Bear ted-dy bear turn a-round ted-dy bear ted-dy bear touch the ground
a   *b*
ted-dy bear ted-dy bear show me your shoe ted-dy bear ted-dy bear
c
how old are you 1 - 2 - 3 - 4 - 5 - 6 - 7 - 8...
d

ACTION

a - player turns around 360°
b - player touches the ground
c - player kicks up one foot
d - player jumps until she or he misses and the chant starts over

Johnny Jump on One Foot

John - ny Jump on One Foot, one foot, one foot.

<u>2nd Verse:</u>   Johnny jump on two foot, two foot, two foot.
<u>3rd Verse:</u>   Johnny jump on three foot..., etc.
<u>4th Verse:</u>   Johnny jump on four foot..., etc.

[Additional verses simile.]

I'm a Liar

I'm a Li-ar jump in the fi-re, fi-re so hot, jump in the pot, he jumped in the pot, the
          a   *a*   *a*

pot so cold, he jumped in the hole, the hole was so nar-row, he jumped in the bar-row, the

bar-row so high, he jumped in the sky, the sky so blue, he part in two

ACTION
a - On the last beat of every measure, the rope is turned high above the jumper's head while he or she continues to jump.

- Bernice Riley

54

Down by the Service Station

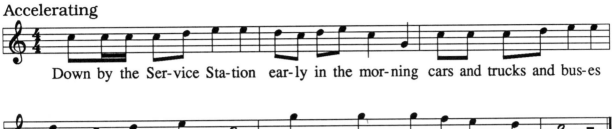

Accelerating

Down by the Ser-vice Sta-tion ear-ly in the mor-ning cars and trucks and bus-es driv-in' for some gas. BEEP BEEP fill it up with gas

ACTION
The rope turns faster and faster towards the end of the chant.

Solomon Agrundy

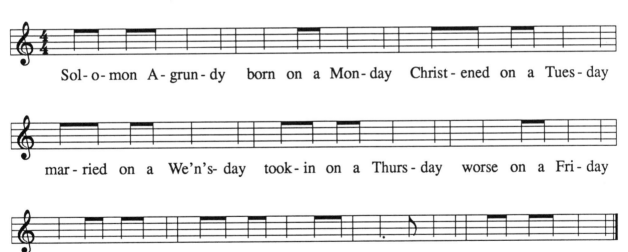

Sol-o-mon A-grun-dy born on a Mon-day Christ-ened on a Tues-day mar-ried on a We'n's-day took-in on a Thurs-day worse on a Fri-day died on a Sat-ur-day bur-ied on a Sun-day and that's the end of Sol-o-mon A-grun-dy

- Jenine Elizabeth Allen
- Jackie Allen, 10 years

Many of the venerable men's clubs that once adorned 5th Avenue in New York have disappeared, but the Salmagundi Club on 47 5th Avenue, founded in 1871 still exists today.

My Mother Your Mother

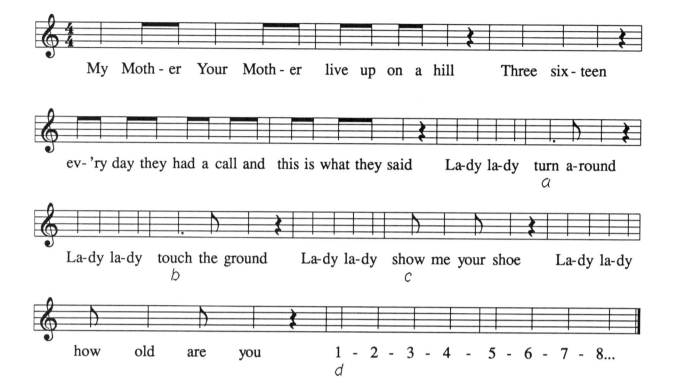

ACTION
a - player turns around 360°
b - player touches the ground
c - player kicks up one foot
d - player keeps jumping until she or he misses and then the game starts over

- Joyce Williams

EBERY FOOL GOT HE OWN SENSE.
　A remarkable bit of philology. A sort of "to each his own." What man, really, can call another "fool"?

Cinderella

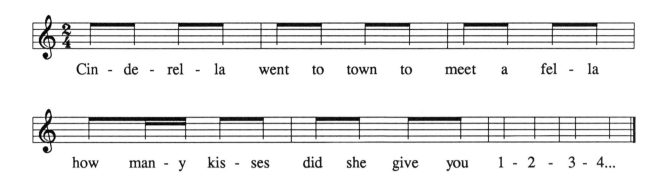

Down By the River

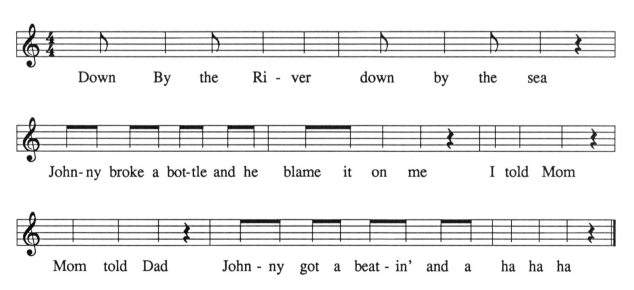

Sally Sally Water

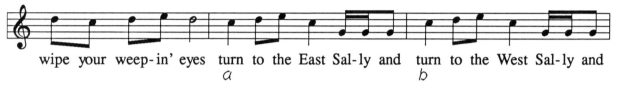
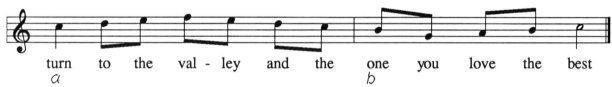

ACTION
a - player jumps and turns 180°
b - player jumps and turns around, back the other way

All Together

ACTION
This game is played with many children jumping at once. When the birthday month of a player is called, he or she runs out.

The Queen of Hearts

The Queen of Hearts she made some tarts tell me the name of your sweet-heart

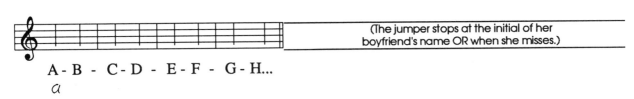
A - B - C - D - E - F - G - H...
a

(The jumper stops at the initial of her boyfriend's name OR when she misses.)

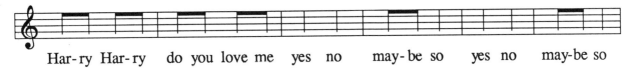
Har-ry Har-ry do you love me yes no may-be so yes no may-be so

yes no may - be so yes no may - be so

2nd verse: What kind of dress do she have? Silver, gold, white, coca-shell.
                                              [repeated until the jumper misses]

3rd verse: How much baby do you have? 1, 2, 3, 4.................[repeated until miss]
4th verse: How much diaper do you have? 1, 2, 3, 4................ "
5th verse: How much bottle do you have? 1, 2, 3, 4................ "
6th verse: How much people be at the wedding? 1, 2, 3, 4...... "
7th verse: How many gifts will you get? 1, 2, 3, 4.................. "
8th verse: What kind of car do you drive? 1, 2, 3, 4................ "

ACTION
a - Hot Pepper - As the rope turns the child jumps only one time after the rope touches the ground instead of twice as usual.

GOOD LIBBIN IS LIKE A' EGG, IF YO' DROP UM YO' CAN' PICK UM UP.

It would be hard to express better: Treasure what you have for, if you lose it, you may never find it again.

Sea Shell Cockle Shell

Sea Shell Cock-le Shell eev-ie iv-y ov-er

Here comes the teach-er with the wal-king stick. All she knows is a-rith-me-tic.

One and one is two. Two and two is four. Now it's time for spel-lin'.

Spell cat. C-A-T. Spell rat. R-A-T. Now it's time for ex-er-cise.

Hands up Hands down Turn a-round Touch the ground. Now it's time for spel-ling.
a   b   c   d

Spell cold. C-O-L-D. Spell hot. H-O-T.

Now it's time for hot pep-per. 1 - 2 - 3 - 4...
e

ACTION
a - jumper holds hands up
b - jumper puts hands down
c - jumper turns around 360°
d - jumper touches the ground
e - Hot Pepper - when the jumper misses, the game starts over.

Fish Fish

Fish Fish Fish in the mar-ket   Ten cents a pound   who don't like it

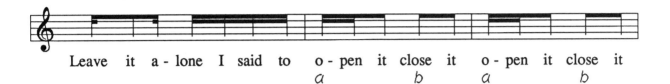

Leave it a-lone I said to   o-pen it close it   o-pen it close it
           a   b   a   b

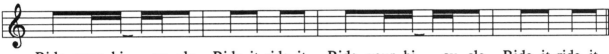

Ride your bi-cy-cle   Ride it ride it   Ride your bi-cy-cle   Ride it ride it
  c   d   c   d

ACTION
a - 'Open it' - jump and spread feet apart
b - 'Close it' - jump and close feet again
c - 'Ride your bicycle' - make a peddling motion with one leg
d - continue jumping again

— Yvette Samuel

NO RAIN, NO RAINBOW.
 Without the problems and sorrows of life
 there can be no success and happiness

Elimination Games and Jokes

1. Here come Tarzan
   Swinging on a rubber band
   Here come Superman
   Boxing in a garbage pan
   And out you may go
   Pick snack and walk right out

   - Roland

2. Batman and Robin flying in the air
   Batman lost his underwear
   Robin say, "I don't care" and
   Robin say, "I'll buy you a new pair"

3. Mickey Mouse was ridin' on a track
   He asked what time it was
   Four o'clock 1- 2- 3- 4
   And out you may go

   - Hazel

4. Eenie meenie minee moe
   Catch a tiger on his toe
   If you want to let him go
   Cup sa sa you may go out

   - Hazel

5. Engine engine number nine
   Goin' down Chicago line
   If the train runs off the track
   Do you want your money back
   Y- E- S spells yes and out you may go

6. Red white an' blue
   The monkey married to you
   He buy a pair of shoe
   In nineteen sixty-two

7. Red white an' blue
   Your boyfriend love you
   He take you to the movie
   And undress you

8. Tarzan went up in a tree
    The tree split and Tarzan shit*
    Cut Tarzan out sa sa
    And out you may go

*[In standard English, 'shit' is considered slang; however in Cruzan, it is not improper or offensive use of the language]

9. Child 'A' asks: "Where are my
        scissors?"
    Child 'B' answers: "I don't know"
        [or in Cruzan:] "Me a' know"
        ["me ain't know"]
    Child 'A' responds: "Your mother married to a shine head lizard"*

*[Translation - someone who is bald; on the island, there are many types of lizards.]

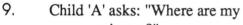

10. a - Give me a high
    b - Give me a low
    c - You're too slow

    ### ACTION
    a - Player 'A' extends his arm up high with hand extended and says,
        "Give me a high." Player 'B' slaps the hand.
    b - Player 'A' extends his arm low with palm open and says, "Give me a
        low." Player 'B' tries to slap, BUT 'A' retracts his hand quickly and says...
    c - "You're too slow."

11. Where's me [my] tamarind
    Come off me [my] mother landin'

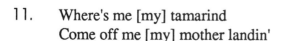

Glossary

ANTINANI — A dragon fly.

BARK — Sick people were "barked". They could be either bathed with a concoction of medicinal plants or have them applied to the stricken area.

BAZADY — Mentally unbalanced, crazy.

BOIA — A baked johnny cake made from corn meal, flour, coconut, bananas, fat pork and black pepper.

BUCKRA — Term used for the white man, particularly the planter.

BUMBA — The boss or driver of field hands on an estate, hence, the headman.

BUMSIE — One's rear or behind, especially a child's.

CAKALAKA — Cockroach.

CHAINY — Shard. A fragment of china or pottery.

CHOOK — To stick or prick. Also to fool. Chook was also a game played with cashew nuts.

COCOBAY — Generally refers to leprosy.

COCKLIE — Generalization for a person.

CONGO ROOT — The plant *Petiveria alliacea*, an abortifacient.

COTACOO — A basket, often carried on the head.

CRAB — The West Indian crab.

CRUZIAN — A native of St. Croix.

DEADIE — Anything used as an obiah symbol, say the frog.

DRIVER	Foreman on a sugar estate.
EH EH	An exclamation denoting surprise, concern. Often followed by "Well, me God!".
FIG	Local name for most varieties of banana.
GUT	Any small stream or stream bed. Example: "Dey washing clothes in the gut".
JACKSPANIARD	Wasp, yellow jacket.
JUMBI	Ghost, spirit who can play tricks on you.
KALALOO	A native soup made of greens and herbs seasoned with ham, fish, conch and crab. A St. Croix specialty.
LIMIN	To hang out with friends, waste time. Derived from the word for an English sailor, "Limey."
MAMPI	Sandfly, midge.
MASSA	Manager, boss, white man.
MAUBI	Soft drink made from bark of *Columbrina reclinata*, or pineapple skin with ginger.
MOKO PUMP	A term denoting a gullible, foolish person. An idiot.
MOKO JUMBI	A masquerader on wooden stilts.
NAYGUR	Negro.
NINYAM	Food.
OBIAH	Witchcraft.
PICKNEE	Black child, offspring.

SALTING	Any main meat or fish dish.
SCUTTLE	A trap door for hurricane use, leading to a cellar or other retreat.
SHEK SHEK	The thibet tree *Albizzia lebeck*; also a frizzy fowl.
SPRAT SAUCE	A fish sauce made with red pepper and lime juice.
SWEET MOUT'	Cajolery, flattery. Buttering up someone.
TAMBRAN	The Tamarind tree, *Tamarindus indica* or its fruit..
TARR	A big marble. Marbles is a game played by kids on the island.
TIZANE	Soft drink made from fruit of soursop.
TRIMITY	A busy body.
TUTU	A conch shell used as a horn.
WANGA	Witchcraft.
WHITEY or WHITEY PEHE	A light complexioned black person. A term of derision.
WIN' T'IEF	A fruit without a kernel, especially a coconut. Stolen by the wind.
YET	To eat. Go "yet" your food.
ZAMBA or SAMBA	A rough cot or bed.

All words in the Glossary have been borrowed from "The Virgin Island Dictionary", through the courtesy of its author, George Seaman.

Omissions:

The following selections have been omitted from this book. The complete collection of songs I have documented can be found in the Archive Library of Congress in sheet music form and on the original live sound field recording (tape # 881999).

1) Johnny Over the Water
2) Some Girls
3) Miss Mary Mack
4) Coca Cola
5) Head and Shoulders
6) Chili Chili Bom Bom
7) China
8) Willowbee
9) Cuman House
10) Fish Fish (alternate version)
11) When Mary Was a Baby
12) When Johnny Was One
13) Under the Blue Bird
14) Punchinella
15) Bluebird
16) Zing Zing Zing
17) London Bridge
18) My Mother and Your Mother
19) Under the Green Bush
20) She She My Baby

These materials may also be purchased directly from the author. For information, contact:

Guavaberry Books
212 Gulph Lane
Gulph Mills, PA 19428
http://www.cyberpg.com

Further Reading:

1) Tossi Aaron, Punchinella 47, ©1978
   Coda Publishing Co., Inc. Philadelphia, PA

2) Adzinyah, Maraire, and Tucker, Let Your Voice Be Heard: Songs from Ghana and Zimbabwe, ©1986
   World Music Press, CT

3) Annual directories, American Orff-Schulwerk Association, Cleveland, OH

4) Fulton and Smith, Let's Slice the Ice, ©1978
   Magnamusic-Baton Inc., St. Louis, MO

5) Jones and Hawes, Step it Down, ©1988 Univ. of GA Press

6) Maureen Kenney, Circle 'Round the Zero, ©1974
   Magnamusic-Baton Inc., St. Louis, MO

7) George H. Seaman, Not So Cat Walk, ©1976
   Crown Printing Co., St. Croix, U.S.V.I., 00820

8) George H. Seaman, Virgin Island Dictionary, ©1976
   Crown Printing Co., St. Croix, U.S.V.I., 00820

DE LONGES' PRAYER GOT AMEN.
How true and wonderful: All things,
both good and evil, come to an end.

About the Author:

KAREN S. ELLIS has a B.S. in Elementary Education from Temple University and graduated Magna Cum Laude. She also has her Certification in Orff Shulwerk from Memphis State University. Ms. Ellis gathered the material for **DOMINO** while teaching elementry school on St. Croix, U.S.V.I. from 1977 - 1979. She was able to use the childrens' songs, chants and games as a framework upon which to develop a highly successful classroom reading curriculum for children whose skills were below grade level. This unique program also motivated and improved the language arts skills of students labelled as emotionally disturbed and learning different. Ms. Ellis resides outside of Philadelphia, with her 13 year-old Cruzan Siamese cat, for whom Guavaberry Books is named.